Advanced Gundog Training

ADVANCED GUNDOG TRAINING

Practical Fieldwork and Competition

Martin Deeley

The Crowood Press

First published in 1990 by
The Crowood Press Ltd
Ramsbury, Marlborough,
Wiltshire SN8 2HR

This edition 1993

© Martin Deeley 1990

British Library Cataloguing-in-Publication Data
A catalogue record for this book is available from the British Library

ISBN 1 85223 771 6

To my wife, Jan.

Typeset by Keyboard Services, Luton, Beds
Printed in Great Britain at The Bath Press

Contents

Acknowledgements

Writing a book does not come easy to me, and I am therefore indebted to my wife for all her support and help, particularly proof-reading. As always, good friends are invaluable, Mike Swan of the Game Conservancy, and Brian and Cherry Alexander, professional photographers who took many of the photographs which have illustrated and enhanced the text.

Introduction

Many handlers, after working with their dogs and realizing the enjoyment and thrill that comes from training and handling, will want to advance to competition and practical work. This book is aimed at helping you to do just that. Whether you want to shoot over your dog, work him for other people or aspire to the high standards of today's field trials, I have drawn from my own and others' experience, information and advice that I feel will help you.

In any job, the basic preparation is the most important thing, no more so than in training a gundog. Without the basic disciplines and exercises being well learnt and becoming natural habits in the dog, there will be little chance of success in advanced work. It is imperative, therefore, that you give your dog a good grounding in the basics of gundog work. If you are uncertain what that grounding is, it would be advantageous to read *Working Gundogs: An Introduction to Training and Handling*, first. If, however, you have decided either to have a dog trained for you to basic standards or to buy a trained dog, the chapter on professional trainers and trained dogs will be of special interest.

Many dog owners choose their dogs and begin training with a particular type of gundog work in mind. There are a variety of jobs at which gundogs excel, including wildfowling, picking up, rough shooting, trialing or other competitive work. As you may not want to teach your dog everything, I have written sections on specific areas, but as you will probably realize, the types of work and the skills required often overlap. Working a good gundog can be addictive and, very quickly, you will be looking at different ways in which you can work with and enjoy your dog. Many Guns have bought a dog as a shooting companion and very quickly relegated the shooting to second best, preferring to handle the dog. I hope that this book will fuel your enthusiasm and interest for the many different ways in which you can work with your dog, and will also provide some of the information to help you make the work that much more enjoyable and fulfilling.

Great pride can be taken in doing things properly, not only for yourself but also for others who will certainly notice (although not always mention it). Neither you nor your dog will ever stop learning, there is always something new to be encountered, a new skill to be learned and, particularly, a greater understanding of each other to be gained. A good dog/handler relationship is built on trust, respect and confidence in each other. Patiently build that relationship as you take your dog to 'finishing school', and polish him to a standard that will enable you to do anything asked of you in the field. If you do this, that respect for each other and the relationship you have can only grow, and when it does you will realize how special and rewarding that man/dog relationship is.

Before taking your dog on to the advanced and practical side of gundog work, do make sure that he is ready both physically and mentally to do so. Although young dogs may seem to be full of bounce and energy, they may not have the fully formed physical make-up to take on the rigours of a shoot day. Shoot days demand stamina and endurance as much as energy, and it is quite easy to damage a tired or weakened body. A tired body is usually reflected in a tired mind, which does not concentrate on you or what is required. When this happens, it is inevitable that the dog will make mistakes or not act as you wish, which can result in bad habits being learned or your losing your patience and teaching him bad habits without realizing it.

It is also worth mentioning at this stage that your dog should be undressed for the part, in other words, he should not be wearing a collar when you are out working him. A collar can so easily get caught up on branches or other obstructions and, if this happens in water, it could be very dangerous.

It is very tempting to take your dog out into the field on the real thing, 'just to see whether he will get on all right and not mind the guns, and to give him a feel for the atmosphere'. The problem is that in getting a feel for the atmosphere, you might be lulled into a false sense of security and allow the dog, or even encourage him, to do certain jobs before he is ready. I have known some people and dogs who have managed to learn together by experiencing everything on the shoot field but, in most cases, problems are caused which will last the dog's lifetime. The most obvious and common one is that the dog becomes too excited and begins to whine and yip – even bark. Once this starts you will have a devil of a job to stop it, if ever. Running in and going out of control are two other com-

mon faults that are caused by lack of basic training and too early an introduction to advanced or practical work.

In the advanced gundog work you are putting greater distances between yourself and your dog. The dog will realize he is outside your area of control if you have not gradually built up to that distance while still maintaining obedience. Build up the distances at which you can control your dog until you are confident that he will respond to your commands wherever he is. Probably the two most important disciplines that your dog should have learned are to stop when commanded and to return when requested. If you can stop your dog in any situation and get him back to you quickly, it will save you a lot of embarrassment and keep him out of danger. He should also walk to heel on and off the lead and be able to carry out seen and unseen retrieves, taking directions: 'Left', 'Right' and 'Get out'. He should enter and retrieve from water and, where required, jump and negotiate obstacles. Obedience and control are the foundations upon which you can build, coupled with the dog's natural instinct to hunt and retrieve, which should not be suppressed but harnessed to work for you.

While your dog is learning his basic exercises and obedience you should be learning about your dog and his mental make-up. To get the best out of your dog, you have to understand what makes him tick, not just the basic animal instincts but his own individual characteristics. Is he a dominant dog or a subservient one? Does he try to please you or himself? Is he easily distracted or is he totally fixed on being with you? Is he a slow or a fast learner? Does he learn the wrong things quickly? Does he sulk or does he accept your control and work with you? There re a hundred more questions you could ask in order to get a picture of your dog and, from the answers, work out how to bring out the best in him. By getting to know your dog, you will learn to read his thoughts by his actions. Very few dogs are good actors – they behave only as themselves. To get the best from your dog you will have to be the actor, playing the part and producing the actions that will get the results you require. You must remember, however, that as you are learning about your dog through watching him in action, he will also be learning about you and recognizing your feelings and emotions through verbal and non-verbal communication. It may be that your dog becomes more skilled at reading you than you are at reading him. If you have an uncomplicated dog who wants to work with you and for you, this can be an advantage, but if the dog is one with a tendency to deviousness and willfulness, then beware!

A day in the field without a well-trained dog to work with me and provide a constant source of companionship, has an emptiness which people who have had dogs will understand. Yes, there are frustrations and moments of despair when you feel that nothing is ever going to go right, but usually when you analyse why those moments have occurred, it is because of something you have done incorrectly. If this book helps you to avoid some of these frustrations and moments of despair, it will have succeeded. There will be times when I have repeated myself but, as all aspects of training and handling a dog are very interrelated, I felt this was necessary.

1 Using a Professional Trainer

For most people, training a dog of the right breeding to an acceptable standard is possible. Not only is it rewarding but it will also enable you to build up a bond with your dog from the very beginning. I would always recommend that anyone who wants a trained gundog should initially consider training the dog himself and only discard the idea after giving serious thought to any reasons for not doing so.

The most common reasons for either buying a trained dog or having a professional train a dog for you are lack of time, ability and experience. I also think that some people should not attempt to train a dog because they do not have the essential character to train successfully (patience being only one of the necessary qualities). Some dog owners may also find that they lack access to training areas or game. City dwellers have often stated this as a problem and I can understand their predicament, the only potential areas for training being busy parks.

Most shooters are looking for and want a dog who is biddable, and trained to a standard that will not disgrace them in the field. Where finance permits, it is possible to have a dog trained for you, or buy one who is already trained. There are advantages and disadvantages to each option, and only you can make the right decision, based on your own feelings and situation.

A professionally trained dog can be expected to walk to heel, come when called by his name or whistled, stop and sit to whistle and command, be steady to shot and falling game, not chase, retrieve when commanded, deliver nicely to hand with a high head carriage and have a gentle mouth. A spaniel should also methodically quarter his ground close to the gun, giving the opportunity for a shot, and sit to flush and/or shot.

Perhaps, for you, one of the most important considerations in picking a dog is the breed-line (perhaps you want a pup from your own bitch or dog). If you opt for having this dog trained, you will have to pick the trainer. With communications and road transport today, there should be no restriction on where you go for the trainer. The investment you will be making in the training of your dog will be far greater than the cost of visiting training kennels. Having said that, it is advantageous if the trainer can train your dog over similar countryside to that which you will encounter during your days shooting. There are a number of professional and semi-professional trainers throughout the country. If you do not know of any, owners of gundogs and gundog societies can often help with some names. Magazines do advertise training kennels but many of the good trainers do not need to advertise, and are booked up for months ahead.

The author with Mr C Burbidge's
'Starblitz Pepper'.

Look for a trainer who has a reputation for delivering the well-trained dog, the trainer whose past clients speak highly of him. Although I will refer to the trainer as male, some of today's trainers are women. The trainer should have experience in training your breed of dog. Some trainers do specialize in one particular breed and you may be better served by a specialist. There is no doubt that recommendations and seeing previously trained dogs are the best methods by which to select your trainer. A good trainer will work hard at building and keeping a reputation, and word of mouth is the usual way by which he will keep and increase his number of clients. Visit the trainer and look at the kennels where your dog will be kept. Make a note of the condition of the kennels and the dogs within them. They should be clean and well cared for. A happy and relaxed atmosphere should prevail and they should not be unduly noisy. Check how many dogs will be in training at any one time, not only clients' dogs but also dogs owned by the trainer. There are only so many hours that a person can work in the day. If you estimate that each dog will require a minimum of half an hour's personal attention a day – training, feeding and socializing – then it does not need a mathematician to determine whether a trainer is 'over-dogged' and therefore unable to give your dog sufficient time.

In discussions with the trainer, you will soon find out whether you are willing to entrust your dog to his kennels. It is important that you build a working relationship with him because there is no doubt that you will want to talk further in the future and, if problems occur at a later stage, to be able to solve them with his help. The trainer should have a business-like approach to dealing with you and you should feel confident not only in his training ability but also in the administration of his business and kennels.

If you are going to send your dog away for training, make sure that he is trainable. You will be spending a considerable amount of money on the training, so take the time and make the effort to get a dog who will benefit from such training and develop into the right type of dog for you. If you have already decided on a trainer, you could ask him for some advice on selecting your dog. If you feel he might sell you one of his own, even though it may not be the right one for you, ask someone else with experience, but if you feel this uncertain about your chosen trainer, is he the right person for you?

Most trainers will want a puppy to be boarded with them at about six to nine months old. It is possible to train the dog when he is older, but by that time, bad habits or problems may already have developed. The older the dog, the more difficult it is to get rid of these problems. Whatever his age, the important thing is that he has not been spoilt in any way for training. I have seen advertisements selling older pups which state that they are 'unspoilt', meaning that training has not started in any way. However, I should be concerned that such pups may have spent their short lives in kennels and have therefore not had early play training or socializing.

In the few months that you have the pup before he goes away to 'boarding school', there are a number of ways in which you can help the trainer bring on a better dog for you. Spend time with the dog and build his confidence around people, introducing him to new surroundings. Get him used to walking on the lead, coming when called and sitting for his dinner when told. Do not allow the dog to go off exploring, either by himself or with other dogs; if you cannot keep an eye on the pup, put him in a kennel or somewhere safe. It is an advantage if the pup is used to kennels before he goes to the trainer. Do not do a lot of retrieving with the pup, no matter how tempting it may be. Certainly, one or two short retrieves a day will get him into the habit and if he brings you objects of his own accord, no matter what they are, take them carefully and praise the dog.

Make sure the other members of your family know how to handle the pup and do not cause any problems for you or the trainer by doing the wrong thing when you are not around. A puppy should not be wrapped in cotton wool, but there is no doubt that those first few months lay the foundation for training to come. If the foundation is a bit crumbly, then some rebuilding may be necessary, and that always takes longer. If in doubt about what to do or not do, talk to your trainer and, if possible, take the pup along so that the trainer can see the type of pup. You should also take your pup's pedigree with you: it will help the trainer get some idea of his background.

When you take the dog along to the trainer, be prepared to answer questions about the dog and the type of work you will want him to do. Give the trainer as much information about his character as possible, including any 'hang-ups' he might have. Particularly mention any problems you may have noticed; do not be afraid to tell the trainer about problems, even if you have caused them yourself. He is going to come up against them during training and, if he is prepared, he may be able to overcome them more quickly by carrying out the training process in a slightly different way. It is a sad fact that many owners only decide to use

a professional trainer when they have made a mess of it themselves. Remedial work takes time and is not always successful, so be honest with the trainer and help him to help you and your dog.

To instil the basics into your dog, the trainer will want him for between four and six months. Some dogs learn quickly, but if you want the good habits really embedded, then plan on this length of time. When asked to train a dog, I usually tell a client that I will want him for at least a month to determine whether I feel the dog has the ability to learn and to make the grade. During that first month, I will also be able to judge my ability to build a relationship with the dog and, specifically, to decide if he is my type of dog – I find it very difficult to train a dog whom I do not like.

Dogs learn at differing rates. They go through peaks and troughs in the learning process, sometimes learning a lesson quickly and at other times creating barriers. Do not rush the trainer, but you should expect to see progress if you visit the pupil after two months. Some trainers do not encourage their clients to visit as it can disturb the dog. I like my clients to visit after two months and then, if they wish, to visit monthly. Generally, after two months in the kennel, I have established a strong enough relationship with the dog so that he does not become stressed when the owner leaves after a visit. I also find that, during the visit, I can do a little owner training in preparation for the time when the dog returns home. The owner can see how the dog is progressing and it also gives us the opportunity to clarify any requirements that did not emerge during the pre-training discussions.

Do not expect training a dog to be cheap. The price will vary from trainer to

13

trainer and sometimes with different areas of the country, but if you want a good job done, it is worth the investment: the dog will be repaying the expense over the next ten years or more.

Most trainers take dogs in over the summer months which means that even though the dog has undergone basic training he may not have had much game shot over him, if any at all. If the trainer is lucky, he may have had a shot at an occasional rabbit or pigeon but the dog will not have experienced a formal shoot day. The transition to live game is not easy and you may have to deal with this yourself. This is the stage at which problems often occur. In some cases, I suggest to the client that he returns the dog to me for a period of four to six weeks in September and October to be introduced to the shooting field. With some clients I have even taken the dog on to their own shoots and worked him in their company to show what the dog can do and, more important, to train them to handle him correctly.

If you decide to buy a trained dog, the one big advantage is that you can see what you are getting. A trainer will demonstrate the dog for you and you should ensure that this demonstration is carried out in such a way that you are confident the dog will do the work you require of him. If possible, have the demonstration on ground unfamiliar to the dog: a dog can perform very well on his own territory, but behave completely differently when run on new ground. Your dog should be trained to work anywhere. It is possible to buy a trained dog who has already had experience of live game and, possibly, one or more seasons in the field. In most cases, the dog will have been kennelled, and if you want him to live in the house you will have to house-train him.

Do not be too concerned about being able to build up a relationship with an older dog. It is very rare that a dog will not take to a new owner who shows him the delights of life, hunting and retrieving. Within two weeks to a month, if you spend time with the dog and share moments of enjoyment together, the dog will very quickly become yours, and will certainly not be concerned about leaving his trainer and old home.

There is probably less risk in buying a trained dog that you can see working, than there is in having your own dog trained and taking a chance on the outcome. It can sometimes be more economical to buy a trained dog but, as it takes approximately twelve months to train a dog up to an acceptable standard and introduce him to the field, do not expect too great a saving. You may be lucky and be able to purchase a dog who was intended for trials and did not quite make the grade, but is of a higher standard than the usual peg-dog or rough-shoot dog. You may also be lucky enough to get a bargain where someone trains one or two dogs on a part-time basis and sells them at a rate below the normal professional fee.

Take your time choosing a trained dog and insist on a full demonstration. If he is being sold as having had live-game experience, ensure that the demonstration is on live game. The cost of the dog should be secondary to determining whether he will fit in with you, your family, your lifestyle, and the type of shooting you will be doing. Carefully assess his temperament and character. A responsible trainer will question you to find out whether you are right for the dog, so do not be affronted if some of the questions seem personal. He should be trying to ensure that the dog gets a good home as much as you are trying to get the right dog.

Whether you have your dog trained or buy a trained one, you must realize that you will have to continue with the dog's development and learn how to handle him. It is so easy to ruin a good dog within a very short time – even days – by thoughtless and careless handling. If you are inexperienced or feel that you could do with some help, ask the trainer to spend some time training you. If this is not possible, you could attend training classes or have private tuition from other trainers. Whatever you do, do not let your lack of ability ruin a good dog and all the hard work that has been put into him.

Do remember that a dog is an animal, not a robot, and that when you take him home there is bound to be some stress. Give the dog time to settle down and become accustomed to his new surroundings and to you. Take him for walks on the lead and spend as much time as possible with the dog so that he comes to know and respect you. Build a relationship based on trust and an understanding that you are the leader now, providing the good things in life, and that you must be obeyed. Do a few of the training exercises that the trainer has shown you each day – this will build both your own and your dog's confidence. Once you have this confidence and a relationship has been established, you can begin to take him into the shooting field but do not expect to be able to do this the day after you have brought the dog home.

If you are making the transition from cold game to live game with the dog, do it gently: do not do too much too quickly. Many Guns ruin their trained dogs before October is out because they push them too early and allow them to do advanced-type work before they are ready. The result is plain to see on many a shooting field – noisy dogs tied to pegs or spaniels who have to be kept on leads all the time. The handlers have let their dogs down, but it is often the trainer who gets the blame.

Look on a trained dog as a solid foundation on which you can build. Make your investment pay by working at it.

2 Advanced Training

POLISHING YOUR DOG

Most people, given the time, effort and a knowledge of what to do, can train a dog up to a standard. What that standard is varies from person to person and dog to dog. Some dog owners are very willing to accept a low standard and will either make excuses for the dog's lack of ability or controllability, or do not appear to notice it at all. It takes considerably more time to get a dog from an average standard to a high standard than it does to take him to the average, or acceptable standard of a shooting man.

Most shooting people will expect a retriever to walk with them (not necessarily at heel), sit at a drive (maybe on a lead) and complete seen retrieves in close proximity to the peg. The average spaniel owner, using him as a traditional questing, flushing dog will expect him to hunt cover without being too concerned about the pattern or ground cover (what the dog misses the handler will kick out), to quest within shooting distance most of the time, to sit or stop to flush and/or shot (not necessarily promptly) and to bring the retrieve back (standard of delivery is not too important). Dogs of this standard will do the job to a certain degree, but how much more satisfying it would be to have a dog who will do the job with a little more finesse. It really is gratifying to be asked to undertake, with your dog, work that others would find impossible: a retrieve over a river to a distant bird that fell after gliding well away from the shooting area; or close hunting in difficult cover for that one elusive bird or rabbit that will provide the shot and the talking point at the end of the day.

What is required is that little bit of polish which seems almost insignificant but which puts the icing on the cake. To do this, your dog should stop promptly on the 'Stop' whistle, wherever he is; look to you for a command; take directions; deal with obstacles; hunt the required area with enthusiasm and, once the retrieve has been found, return directly to you; he should deliver the bird with a high head carriage, allowing you to take it with one

Make the dog wait while you go through a gate . . .

. . . it is safer and only polite to do so.

hand. In addition, a spaniel should hunt for game within killing range of the gun, making sure that no potential game-holding cover is missed; make the best use of wind and scenting conditions; sit promptly to the flush or the shot from the gun; and wait until commanded to retrieve. All of this should be done without barking, whining or yipping.

A well-finished dog will not only be a pleasure to watch and to work with, but will also provide you with more shooting or game in the bag by employing more refined and highly tuned gundog skills. If you are considering competition, either tests or trials, polish is essential to give you any opportunity of winning awards. Some faults will not only incur penalties in points or grading, but many even eliminate you from a competition. A high standard of performance and 'finish' may make the difference which puts you and your dog among the top awards.

There are always reasons for standards being set, and although some people have been heard to ridicule finer points of gundog work (particularly distance control and handling), the higher the standard of your dog and the more polished he is, the more likely you are to succeed at a job.

In my book *Working Gundogs*, I discussed the basics of gundog training and touched on the advanced work. If you have mastered these basics, you will be on the way to a more polished gundog. However, as with all things in life, not everything goes as planned and problems occur. These problems can be a real stumbling block even to the point of creating a barrier, which not only arrests develop-

Working in company at training classes. Do not rush the job. Spend time developing a good delivery. Encourage the dog to raise his head by rubbing his chest and under his chin and also by not grabbing at the dummy.

ment in one particular aspect of the training, but also affects other aspects, causing more problems. I will identify some of the more common problems and offer possible solutions, and will expand further on the more advanced training techniques.

There is no exact stage at which you start 'polishing' your dog: training is one continuous process, which commences the moment you get your dog. Every dog is different and so you will have to study your particular dog and read from his actions what makes him tick. Watch and study his mannerisms and actions and identify what he is good at and what his weaknesses are. Even pups from the same litter can be as different as chalk and cheese and therefore require different approaches to achieve the same results.

Two of my own spaniel pups are good examples of how they can differ. The dog pup not only differed from his sister in

size – he was tall and long bodied, she small and close coupled – but also in his personality and naturally exhibited skills. The dog pup loved picking up objects and bringing them to me, very little encouragement being required, and when he arrived with a retrieve he was naturally inclined to sit. A little rub of the chest and he lifted his head for the delivery. Once the retrieve had been taken he was then quite happy to be with me. This was a good strength to work on, but his weakness was that he was not a natural hunter with a natural pattern. He ran in straight lines bouncing up and down looking all about him, and was more interested in objects he saw than in getting his nose down to search for scent. My main task with this dog, therefore, was to get him to hunt with a good pattern while still maintaining his interest in retrieving.

His sister was a natural hunter from the

very beginning: she seemed to have an instinct for finding game and was always busy searching every piece of cover for potential finds. The fact that most of this hunting was done on game-free ground did not concern her – if it was ground, it was made to be hunted, and cover was made to be investigated. Her weakness was that she could not sit still, not even to be praised or to deliver a retrieve. Full of the 'fidgets' and in perpetual motion, getting her to sit and stay took endless patience. When delivering a dummy, which she would happily carry, she would run around and jump up at me so fast, bouncing away when you reached down to her, that developing and co-ordinating the correct responses was very difficult. The big strength that they both shared was their responsiveness and willingness to work with me, without which I would have been lost.

In order to train a dog, not only must you be willing to train him but he must be attentive and willing to learn. Some dogs have a natural, almost fanatical willingness; there are some in which you can develop an interest and willingness; and then there are others that have no desire to learn and work with you. There is a saying that there is no such thing as a bad dog, only bad trainers. Do not believe it – there are some bad dogs, dogs that have not got the breeding, character and natural desire to please. It should always be remembered that, to be really successful at training a dog, you must like him and he must like you – that relationship is essential.

In basic training there is considerable emphasis on exaggeration and voice tones. As you move on to the more advanced training you should attempt to quieten down your approach and build on the basic commands and signals through experience and association. There still needs to be shades of 'light and dark' in your voice and whistle tone, but as your dog begins to respond you can reduce the volume and amount of signals given. It is quite surprising how often the dog does not even require a verbal signal – facial expressions can show pleasure and disapproval which your dog will respond to. A pleased expression may be all the praise he requires once he has moved on to 'University', but remember this is dependent upon the dog and his character. Get to know your dog well and find out what will produce the desired results, then you can make the best use of these stimuli.

In the early months, not only should you be developing your dog but also recognizing those little characteristics and facets of his personality that can either cause problems or help you achieve. Some characteristics are created by you and others are natural. Eye contact, where your dog looks to you and shows interest and enthusiasm, comes from a natural characteristic, but can be further developed or enhanced through your actions and training. Within the training programme, you may make a mistake, correct the dog in error or, worse still, lose your temper. This can quite easily create a problem characteristic, and one which is far more difficult to eradicate than it was to create. Like humans, the memories of fear and pain last longer than the ones of pleasure; and someone reprimanding us unfairly goes deeper and hurts more than it does when that person says 'well done'. In the majority of situations, if you have developed the correct relationship, your dog will be trying to please you. If he is acting incorrectly it is more than likely because he does not know what to do to be correct in that precise situation. You should know your dog well enough by this stage to determine whether he is working for you and with you or 'trying it on'. Your reaction should be governed by this knowledge.

To get the best out of your dog in the advanced stages, he must have had a thorough grounding in the basics. It is so tempting to try to progress to the more interesting advanced stages, but without the basic lessons being thoroughly learnt, you are bound to come up against problems. Never be too proud to go back to the basics if you find that your dog has developed a problem.

You may also find that your dog has learnt the basics but can only perform them in a particular location. Many of us have difficulty in varying the ground over which we train our dogs and, owing to time and convenience factors, may use only one particular piece of land. This, in itself, creates problems as the dog may associate what he has been asked to do with a specific piece of terrain. By using the same country path or ride to do, perhaps, an unseen retrieve or left- and right-hand signals, your dog will become conditioned into performing the required actions not by watching you but in automatic response to the place in which he does it.

I own five acres of grass and woodland with a small lake, where I can train my dogs. Many people say that I have all the facilities available at my fingertips, but dogs that perform perfectly on this ground can become quite confused when I take them to a new training ground. It is not until they have been to a number of new training areas that they begin to react totally to you and gain confidence regardless of where they are being run. The solution is, of course, not to be lazy — make an effort to take your dog to new and differing grounds.

If you consider the various types of ground cover and terrain over which you will expect your dog to work and then look for similar training areas, your dog will undoubtedly benefit. Root crops, stubble, ditches, gateways, thick hedges and many other workplaces cause difficulties, particularly if they are unfamiliar. By familiarizing your dog with these during the training sessions and creating a confidence in your dog, problems will be minimized.

As well as polishing your dog to a high standard and further developing his ability, it is important that you also polish yourself. Handling is a skill which, if developed to a high degree, can bring good results from an average dog. An understanding of situations, an ability to read the dog and experience of handling both, together with a natural flair, can take you to peaks in the working partnership. Not only must you learn how to deal with situations requiring an understanding of the practical aspects of dog work, but you must also develop an understanding of your dog's behaviour patterns. Learn how to read your dog through his actions, posture and eyes so that you can obtain the required reactions. You should be working with him to make things happen, not waiting until something happens and then reacting to it. Experience which is learnt from and stored as knowledge will enable you in the future to look ahead and foresee the right things to do and the problems to be avoided. By continuing to build on your own skills, experience and knowledge, you will be able to work better with your dog, providing a greater opportunity for him to do what you require.

In any working partnership, not only does there have to be respect but also a belief and confidence in each other's ability. The trust and understanding has to be mutual. You can develop this further by ensuring that you are consistent in your actions and commands, by not acting irrationally and by assisting your dog in exercises which he finds pleasurable. When your dog believes you and reacts to your commands immediately, confidently knowing that you are correct, control becomes total. You, however, must be able to interpret your dog's actions and know when to control and when to leave him to work things out for himself. A dog's senses are more finely tuned than his handler's: when a dog finds scent, only he knows where the scent is stronger, which direction game has taken, or where it is to be found. Experience will teach him to become skilled at reading and interpreting scent; your skill will come from knowing when to leave alone and when to give that little extra assistance that will put him on to the right line once more.

Today, as at any time in the past, a gundog of any breed has to be a hunter. Unfortunately, many trainers (particularly of retrievers) do not develop the hunting ability in their dogs; instead they turn them into 'guided missiles' which will work only in the direction the handler commands, and which need to be helped every stage of the way to the 'find' of the game. Polishing is a fine balance between control and natural ability, individual style, drive and character and trained finishing; it is the ability of both dog and handler to make everything look easy and comfortable.

DEVELOPING EYE CONTACT

Watch any good dog and his handler and you will notice one important feature of the partnership: when the need arises the dog looks to the handler for guidance and support. In fact, not only does he look *to* the handler, he also looks *at* him – the eye contact is forming an important part of dog/handler communication.

With some dogs, this is a natural inbuilt characteristic – they want to be part of your pack and look to you for leadership and guidance. It is, however, easy to lose this through poorly thought out training and handling. With every dog you need to work at developing the rapport that will result in good eye contact.

Eye contact is a strange thing. When we first start to train a dog to retrieve, it is considered advisable not to look the dog directly in the eye. By staring at the dog, it may appear that we are challenging the animal and this, by making him wary, may cause him to drop the dummy or to circle round you. Many books tell us to look at a space between or above the eyes. How we can do that when the dog is a distance away from us I do not quite know! It certainly becomes easier when the dog is closer. Some books tell us to hide our eyes under the peak of a cap and wait for the dog to come into view. In both cases, the aim is to avoid frightening the dog through staring.

There is no doubt that in the animal kingdom, the eyes are a very important means of communication. Watch any animal threatening another: it is not just body posture and noise, but also the eye that is employed. Open, glaring eyes are threatening, challenging, aggressive. The handler who does not look directly into his dog's eyes will avoid sending these confrontational signals. When an animal is pleased, content and showing friendliness, the eyes slightly close, the mouth turns up and the face softens. Try using these signals when your dog approaches. A smile will be recognized as being friendly and non-aggressive, and such signals of pleasure and friendliness will enable you to keep eye contact with your dog and enhance the working relationship.

Dog handlers experience times of intense concentration. This often results in tension which will show on your face. The dog, recognizing these signs, then reacts out of character; this increases your tension and you are on the downward spiral. So, make the effort and smile (or at least relax your face) when the dog is doing things well. Concentrating on relaxing your facial expression may actually help you to relieve your tensions and reduce the likelihood of your losing your temper, which could be disastrous. By relaxing and softening your expression, eye contact becomes easier, particularly with a sensitive dog. Good eye contact is achieved by a combination of animal communications and feelings, plus some training.

No one can expect to build a relationship with a dog without spending time in his company and what is done in that time is crucial. The dog should be looking to you for guidance and leadership. If you allow him to become too independent and self-confident, the situation can arise where he does not feel that he needs you and therefore does not look to you. From the moment you obtain your puppy, you are building a relationship with the dog. Together you will be developing personality and character. If you develop an independent and self-willed dog, you will create problems for yourself and, likewise, if your dog becomes over-sensitive and nervous. You have to achieve the correct balance.

Sitting calmly with your dog is good therapy for both of you. Stroke him under the chin encouraging him to look into your face. Keep his attention with your voice and facial expression and keep his head facing towards you with careful use of the hands. This also applies when the dog has retrieved to you. After taking the retrieve, do not allow him to move away immediately, either to start working again or, worse still, to sniff aimlessly. Even looking around indicates a lack of interest in you. Keep the dog sitting in front as you praise him, and only allow him to move on your instruction. Only give instructions when the dog is purposely looking at you, because then he will learn to look to you for that instruction which he really wants to see. In fact, if there is a secret to eye contact, it lies in keeping the dog so keen and enthusiastic (and therefore happy) that he will not want to take his eyes off you in case he misses anything which would be enjoyable.

With a young dog in particular, use a very quiet voice when giving normal situation instructions, and a quiet whistle blow. This encourages the dog to be more attentive – he has to concentrate more on you in order not to miss them. Concentration on the handler and eye contact work hand in hand.

Teach the dog to associate looking at you with activities that give him pleasure. Your dog should enjoy retrieving so, before throwing the dummy, get his attention, hold it with your eyes, and then throw. There are a variety of ways to keep your dog's attention on you: hiding behind trees when he is not looking; walking down a different path to the one the dog has taken; and using the occasional attention-catching noise. All these must be followed by praise when the dog reacts positively. If you give your dog a biscuit, hold it level with your eyes so that the dog has to look to your face to see the biscuit before you give it.

There are some dogs who are very

Encourage his interest in you by doing things the dog enjoys and do not let anything else distract him.

difficult to create eye contact with. This may be owing to nervousness, when they are worried about looking into your eyes; independence, even arrogance, which is part of their character; or interest in happenings and objects other than you. If you can identify why the eye contact is not there, you can adjust your training accordingly. The nervous dog needs to be reassured and his confidence built up. Look at him with a softened eye, stroke and hold his head towards you for short periods and build up the trust between you. When dealing with a nervous dog, be careful not to make any mistakes, lose your cool or overdo the contact in the early stages. The independent, arrogant dog is the most difficult. Where this is part of his natural character, you almost have to force the dog to look at you. I have found with these dogs that a high degree of obedience and discipline training – almost to the extent of 'square bashing' and 'brain

Become the centre of attention, where nothing and no one else matters to the dog except you and your wishes.

23

Praise your dog and encourage him to
look at you.

washing' – does help. The dog is not allowed to do anything in the early days unless you give the command and allow it. He has to respond instantly to the simplest command and nothing more is done until the dog looks at you for the next instruction. I particularly try to keep a dog of this type guessing – in other words, I never let him know what is coming next. The command to stop, which is generally the least interesting to this type of dog, is followed by an interesting and even exciting exercise.

Not only are you working at eye contact but also at becoming the centre of attention, which is not easy with a dog of this character. During the 'square bashing', which includes walking to heel at varied paces, sitting, staying and coming when called, I ensure that the dog looks and pays attention all of the time. My commands tend to be a little sharp, even brusque. If his attention wanders, I use my voice in warning or even give a sharp tap on the nose, making sure that I gain his full interest. These dogs are not easy to work with, but if you are to reach a good working relationship, you will have to develop a strong leadership which can be reinforced through this eye contact. I have often found with this type of dog that, although he can do wrong through wilfulness, when he moves into the field he will pull off the most astounding retrieves of runners or difficult birds.

The dog who is more interested in his surroundings is fairly easy to build eye contact with. Again, you have to become more interesting than anything else around him and develop in him an obedience which makes him respond to your smallest signal.

Eye contact starts from the moment you have a puppy and, if you have bred the pups yourself, make sure that they are socialized, handled and played with from the beginning.

Use your eyes to help you control your dog: soft smiling eyes to encourage and say 'Yes, you're doing all right'; wide glaring eyes to threaten and say 'No!'.

Just as your dog can read your eyes, you should learn to read your dog's. You should be able to recognize attentiveness, affection, lack of interest, fear, concern, submission, confusion. All of these are important feelings since they influence your dog's readiness and ability to learn and progress. Being able to identify them will help you to train your dog more effectively. Adapt your training where necessary and develop the mutual understanding which will create that lasting bond between you and your dog.

OBEDIENCE AND CONTROL AT A DISTANCE

In the training sessions, you will often find that you are alone with your dog. Because of this, dummies are never thrown further than a distance of perhaps thirty or forty yards (if you have a strong right arm), and hidden dummies are rarely placed further away than this often owing to laziness – we do not want to walk too far. Your dog is therefore trained to perform at short distances from you and, if he does this well, you presume that he can work just as well at greater distances. This is not the case: a dog needs to be given experience of working at increasingly greater distances, ensuring that he is under control and obeying you at each step further away.

At distance, the signals your dog has to read and respond to are the whistle which stops him, and the hand signal which gives directions. These signals are used in conjunction with each other to direct your dog into a particular area where a retrieve can be found. To maintain the control that you have at short distances, gradually increase the distance between you and the dog in short steps. Do some of the basic direction exercises at greater distances from you, sending the dog left, right and back and sitting him at increasing distances from your signal. The 'Get Back' or 'Get Out' command can often cause a problem as dogs want to go left or right rather than back. Some dogs also come back towards you before going right or left when given the right or left signal. The main causes of this are lack of confidence and lack of experience. The dog gets a picture in his mind of what he thinks is required

and does it every time. You somehow have to break this fixation, this habit, by guiding the dog into the correct action and making sure that it becomes the habit.

Progression from one signal to another should be as simple and as natural as possible in order to help your dog take the correct direction. For example, if you are going to send the dog to the right, give the stop signal with your right hand before then pushing it out horizontally in the right-hand signal. Conversely, when you are going to give a left hand signal use the left hand to give the stop signal prior to giving the left direction signal. If the dog comes towards you when moving either left or right, make use of paths or country rides to guide him at right angles, and do not place the dummy so far away that the

Get your dog working at increased distances and give good clear signals
– 'Get Out'.

Use natural objects to help guide your dog – here using a hedge.

dog cannot see it and therefore move as you wish. To develop the correct action for unseens, make use of country-path crossroads, placing the dummy a short distance away from where the dog is to be sat (with the dog left in the car or kennel at this time). Bring out your dog, sit him at the centre of the crossroads, and give the signal directing him on to the hidden dummy. Initially, stand only a short distance away from the dog, but gradually increase it until you can give the signal at upwards of 100 metres and obtain the correct response. I often find that using the same crossroads for the hidden dummy and the seen dummy is initially advantageous as the dog is confident of success in that place.

To make a dog get out from you, going directly away, again country paths can be of help in guiding the dog, as can hedgerows and rows between crops and fences. Increase the distance between

you and your dog but leave the distance between your dog and the dummy the same, so that he gains confidence in spinning around and succeeding in finding the dummy very quickly directly behind.

One of the main problems which occurs once your dog is beginning to understand the signals at a distance, is that he will begin to anticipate. He sees your right hand up and guesses you are going to send him right, so he moves in that direction before you signal. If you were going to send the dog back, with the pushing signal, he has therefore gone wrong. So, be ready for this and, using 'Stop' whistle and voice, make sure that your dog does not move until you signal. If he does, and gets to the dummy before you can stop him, back-track and move closer to the dog where you can exercise control to ensure that he does not move until you tell him to. Build up this exercise until you

Picture how your dog sees you and make sure your signals are
clear and unambiguous.

can put out hidden dummies to the right
of, left of and behind the dog and then,
from distances of 100 metres and more,
send him to the one you require.

There are also different types of arm
and body movements you can perform in
giving a hand signal. Each one, if performed consistently in a particular situation, will develop the dog's ability to
read the signal and help him with the find.
Shooting the arm out in a swift, vigorous
movement while leaning the body in the
same direction, is used to send the dog for
a long distance in the required direction.
A gentle arm movement, maybe with just
a slight waving of the hand, is used to
send him a short distance and says 'take it
easy'. The hand held lower, moving down
to the ground, with a 'patting' motion
asks the dog to move just slightly in that
direction and search around where he is.
Practising these signals as you go through
retrieving exercises will familiarize the

dog with the actions and create that extra
control which enables you to help the
dog.

As well as hand signals, voice can also
be varied in conjunction with each signal,
to convey even more meaning: 'Get Out!'
in a hard forceful tone to get the dog
moving and to push him back quickly;
and 'Hi Looost' in a soft, gentle tone to
tell him that he is about right and to
persevere in hunting carefully where he is.
Some handlers introduce other words to
convey these meanings, such as 'Easy',
'Carefully' or 'There'. If you do this,
make sure that you remain consistent and
do not start stringing a load of different
words together, which in the end will
mean nothing to the dog and will only
encourage him to ignore you. When the
dog is at a distance I often wonder
whether he can actually hear vocal commands and whether they are actually
necessary. The sound of your own voice is

'Hunt carefully and not too far to the right' can also be used to direct a
hunting spaniel, as well as a retriever.

'Hunt carefully to the left.'

'Hunt just in front of you. Easy!'

probably more reassuring in your own mind than it is of benefit to the dog. It is also worth remembering that too many actions saying the same thing can be confusing to a dog and it is sometimes more effective to use just whistle and hands with no verbal commands.

To help the dog to see the signals, some handlers may find holding a handkerchief in the hand which is giving the signal can help to catch his attention. I have seen other handlers roll up their sleeves so that the white of their hands is extended by their arms or shirt sleeves. With some dogs this does help; with others I have seen little effect. There are time when the hands of the handler are against a light background such as sky and, looking at them from a distance, all that really stands out are the dark sleeves, not the hands or handkerchief. I often feel that, rather than giving any real advantage to

the dog, such methods are of most benefit to the handler whose confidence is increased by believing that the dog can see better. If you feel that it is of benefit, then do it because even if it only helps you to be confident, it will make you a more proficient handler.

When you reach the stage where you want to give your dog long retrieves, it can be of great help to have an assistant who can throw or place dummies at the required distances. Working with a friend who is also keen on dog training, or attending training classes, is the best way to approach this problem. If you use someone who is a friend and has no knowledge of dog training, you must ensure that they know what you want, what they can and cannot do and, although it sounds ludicrous, that they can throw a dummy accurately (so many people cannot). If you think carefully

When sending a dog away from your side, it can help if you use your whole body and legs, as well as your arm, to give him a clear direction. Notice the very forceful, driving Send Away in this instance.

A white handkerchief can help the dog to see your hand signals better, if you are against a dark background.

about this part of the dog's development you can start to create a multitude of situations and exercises to build experience and improve control. Your dog will also begin to realize that the retrieve does not always get launched from your hand. Game does not flush from your hand and therefore the dog has to learn to watch the line of the game from the flush and, in the case of a bird, look for the fall. If you or your assistant uses a gun and points it in the direction of the thrown dummy, your dog will learn to look for direction from the pointing of the gun. To begin with always keep the gun pointing in the direction of the thrown dummy for an extended period of time.

The ability of your dog to mark at distance is essential to enable him to get to the fall area as quickly as possible without disturbing game. Marking is very much a natural ability in some dogs who seem to do it effortlessly. In others, it has to be developed gradually but, once learnt, it makes all the difference between success and failure on a retrieve. Even if you think your dog has marked a retrieve, always make sure that you give him a clear, directional send-off movement with your arm. Not only will it reassure the dog that it is the right retrieve for him to fetch, but it will also build up his confidence in taking send-off directions from you when going out for an unseen. An additional command that some handlers use is 'Mark' which, together with a pointing arm, tells the dog to watch the fall of a dummy and remember it. This is a useful attention-getting command, and it encourages the dog to concentrate on the particular retrieve that he will be sent for and which he might otherwise miss. For example, by using the command, a dog can be turned around at heel for a bird that falls

A clear direction signal for a young dog
and 'Mark' to bring attention to a dummy
falling ahead.

behind the line. If you do decide to use the 'Mark' command, be careful not to send your dog too quickly after giving it, as he will soon associate the command with being sent, and running-in could result.

Many dogs develop the habit of looking at their handlers after they have marked a retrieve to look for the 'Fetch' command. This can result in the dog losing his mark although, with experience, he will learn to remember it. My own experience is that a dog who does this is less likely to run-in than one whose total concentration is on the retrieve, the slightest movement or word triggering the run-in. If you are lucky enough to have a natural marker who continues to watch the fall and remains steady, make a point of giving the 'Fetch' command and signal alongside the head where the dog can get the message and still remain transfixed on the mark. Getting the dog to look at you may result in mis-marking.

STOPPING ON THE WHISTLE

The art of moving a dog to the required area where he can then be set hunting to find a dummy, consists of moving him in squares – right, left, back and occasionally forward. To do this, the dog must not only obey hand signals but must also stop promptly on the whistle and look at you.

Dogs have to be trained to stop on the whistle at increasing distances from the handler. Without this ability to stop the dog on the whistle, it is impossible to control and direct him effectively. From early puppy days your dog should have been taught to stop and sit on the single whistle blast. Once your dog has learnt

that one blast means 'Sit', use the whistle to sit the dog whenever it is required, particularly when it is followed by something pleasurable. Too often, the 'Sit' whistle is a negative signal, instructing the dog to stop what he is doing and, occasionally, to tell him that he is doing wrong and that he is in trouble. Try to make the 'Sit' whistle a more positive signal, one that means something pleasurable is going to happen next, or one that says, 'Look to me for guidance – I'm going to help you do something pleasurable'.

A retrieve is a pleasurable experience and, once your dog is stopping to the whistle and steady, you can begin to follow the 'Stop' whistle with a dummy being thrown. As part of direction training, this can be thrown to the left or right or over the dog's head and then, after waiting, sending the dog with the appropriate signal. The situation to beware of here is one where your dog anticipates what is going to happen, so occasionally pick up the dummy yourself or throw out two dummies and send him for the one he is least expecting to fetch. Once the dog has retrieved one dummy, pick up the other yourself, either leaving him on the drop or walking him to heel.

Most dogs will at some time ignore the whistle, usually because they are carrying out an action which, in their minds, takes priority over your command. You must not allow this to happen. Once your dog understands the 'Stop' whistle, he must stop at the first blast – two or three blasts later is not good enough because soon he will not be stopping at all. If he does ignore your whistle, rush out towards the dog and, using a gruff voice and the whistle, make sure he does sit. If the dog is being strong willed and not sitting, grab hold of him and give him a shaking or, if the dog is too big for you to pick up, push him down to the ground blowing a long whistle blast in his ear and then making him sit. If you feel that this is too strong a method of dealing with your type of dog, attempt to make him sit at distances where he will obey and gradually build them up. Any slowness in sitting should bring from you an attention-getting call or action (such as throwing a dummy) and the 'Sit' command once more. Your dog will begin to realize that the pleasure of a retrieve or praise only comes once he has sat – do not take second best and do not give up.

It does not matter what distance the dog is from you; you must ensure that he knows you can be in contact with him and will not accept second best. Once the dog has sat to the whistle, praise him

Whistle, concentration and a clear hand signal to stop the dog at distance. In this instance a young dog is on the lead, so you can totally concentrate on the one being handled.

and give him something pleasurable to do. The 'Stop' whistle, either close up or at a distance, is essential to good gundog work and, although you do not want to destroy any drive or initiative in your dog from using it too often, it must be obeyed when you blow it. It is quite easy to provide excuses for your dog not obeying at a distance, the most obvious being that he cannot hear the whistle. With some whistles this may be possible if the tone and pitch is a low one. I personally do not like staghorn ones for this reason, but other handlers find them ideal. Weather conditions and crops, such as rustling sugar beet, which the dog may be working in can also create problems with the hearing of the whistle, but do not be fooled into making excuses for your dog too often. Your dog's hearing is much more acute than your own, and he can hear a lot more than you realize, particularly high-frequency whistles. Different dogs react to different whistles, and it may be that you have to experiment to find one that gains the best reaction from your dog.

Some trainers recommend using two whistles, one a thunderer (football referee's whistle), to stop the dog. There is no doubt that this particular whistle has a very commanding blast and, in the dog's mind, there can be no confusion if that whistle is used just to stop him. My problem is that I find two whistles difficult to handle. I usually walk along with one whistle in my mouth – always prepared – and to have to change it to a second one when I want to stop the dog (which can be a very quick, spontaneous decision) creates too much fumble and time lapse for me. Whether you use one or two whistles, do not let the whistle become an excuse for your dog disobeying. Changing the type of whistle may not be the answer o your problem – there is no such thing as a magic flute.

JUMPING

In my part of the country, most fences are topped with barbed wire and in some cases this is a single strand above pig wire netting. I am therefore very careful about sending my dog for a retrieve where it has fallen on the other side of a fence, unless I can see that it is safe. Some trainers expect their dogs to clear fences of any height, barbed wire and all, and have told me that once a dog has caught himself a couple of times, he will learn to jump clear. I am afraid that I do not take the chance, although I do teach my dogs to jump as it is essential that they do so if they run in competitions.

In trials, most judges will not expect your dog to jump a dangerous fence and will look for a way around it, even to the point of telling you to go up to the fence with your dog and lift him over. This is very much the case in spaniel trials, but I have seen some retrievers asked to complete quite difficult fences in their trials.

Dogs do enjoy jumping and if you have taught your dog correctly, you should have little difficulty with increasing the distance at which you can command him to jump a fence or negotiate something like a high bank or stone wall. There will be times when you cannot go forward to your dog to help him negotiate an obstacle, for example, when

A dog may have to jump a fence into thick cover and then work on his own initiative out of sight, particularly in a test.

there is a river between you. You should therefore build up the distance at which you can send your dog over a fence on both a seen and an unseen retrieve. If you have taught the dog the word 'Over', he will know, when given the command, that he is expected to go to the other side of an obstacle such as a fence, wall or river. Initially, build up the distance on seen retrieves and then introduce unseen retrieves when your dog is confident with normal unseens and with jumping at a distance from you.

In many competitions, your dog will be expected to jump, and often at a distance from you. In a Novice test this is usually on a seen retrieve, but with an Open test this could easily be an unseen and the dummy could be well back from the fence or wall. In this case, your dog will have to get out from the fence, which is not too bad a task if you can see through it; if it is a wall, your dog will have to work out of sight on his own initiative. One of the most difficult retrieves over a jump or even on the near side of a jump is one that lies at the foot of the fence. In this situation, the dog takes off, lands away from the base of the fence and never hunts that area. If your dog is a keen jumper and goes over without command it is quite easy to miss this retrieve. One who will hunt all the ground before the fence and not cross over it until commanded will have an advantage.

Teach your dog to jump and respond to the 'Over' command at a distance, but do make sure that you know what type of jump it is so as to avoid putting him in danger. I know of one wall which looks quite low and easily negotiated from the field side, but the blind side has a drop of about ten feet on to a hard road. A keen, enthusiastic dog leaping that wall could very easily damage himself badly.

THE RETURN AND DELIVERY

By watching your dog and reading his actions you should be able to avoid a number of problems before they can occur. However, not everything goes perfectly. You may do something wrong, or the dog may develop or have an in-built problem which you will then have to overcome. Many problems occur in the return and delivery of a retrieve which, if done correctly, should involve a clean, smooth pick up, a fast, direct return to the front of the handler and a sitting delivery with the head held high and the retrieve forward to be gently released into your hand when you grasp it. Following this delivery, the dog should remain sitting until you give him a further command.

There are many problems that can occur and, naturally, there are a number of solutions to each problem. Only from your knowledge of the problem and the character and behaviour of the dog can you decide on the right one. If we take some of the more common problems and explain some of the possible solutions, it will help you to determine your own approach.

With the pick up and return, it must be remembered that not all dogs are the same. Some dogs will carefully pick up a retrieve, adjusting it on the ground so that they can get the right comfortable hold for the return – do not confuse this with 'mouthing', where the dog is really playing about with the retrieve and not attempting to pick it up. At the other extreme, some dogs are like the Lancers, and pick up the retrieve on the run with a flamboyance and swiftness that defies belief. The dog to watch out for is the mouther or the blinker (one that knows

A good sitting delivery with the head up
— the bird can be taken with one hand.

the dummy is there but ignores it). Some dogs go through a mouthing stage when you introduce rabbit skin or feather covered dummies and also when you move on to cold and then warm game. The new texture and scent either excites them or makes them unsure and, sometimes, they will even refuse to pick up a new type of retrieve. Even though your dog may have gone through all the stages and been introduced to game, he may balk or play about with new species of game which he has not carried before. Woodcock, snipe and teal may cause picking-up problems, and some dogs will lick warm rabbits rather than bring them back the first time they encounter them.

Be aware that this can happen and, if it does, do not panic – it can only make matters worse. A dog who does not pick up dummies cleanly can be encouraged by voice or whistle to return the moment he reaches the dummy. If it has been well ingrained in the dog that he must return when called and if he also has a keen desire to hold the dummy, he will usually pick up the retrieve quickly and return to you with it. If there is a reluctance to pick up the dummy and, upon being re-called, the dog returns without it, do not throw the dummy too far next time and encourage him with your voice to 'Fetch it'. Sometimes you may need a gentle tone, at others a firm tone to get the result, but once the dog is returning, praise him and let him know how pleased you are.

Patience is a key word with a dog who is a problem retriever – work at it but do not rush or lose your cool. If you frighten a sensitive dog while working on a retrieving problem, you could put him off retrieving for a long time. Retrieving should be fun, and by your attitude and praise of the dog, you can make it fun.

Occasionally, the canvas dummy is not interesting enough for a dog, in which case, you may obtain the desired results if you use a rabbit-skin dummy, which is much more interesting. I know of trainers who do not like to use a rabbit-skin dummy too early, but if and when it achieves the desired result and makes the dog enthusiastic to retrieve, you can then go back to the canvas dummy. I have found skin dummies particularly useful to encourage dogs to enter cover, such as brambles – the more tempting smell helps to overcome their initial reluctance.

The canvas dummy itself can create problems in the pick up for dogs who are especially gentle in the mouth. This is made worse when the dummy has become wet or slimy with saliva. Try to keep your dummies dry and help the dog to learn how to hold by using a well-designed dummy that he can grip and balance. For dogs with this problem, I find that covering a standard canvas dummy with an old woollen sock enables them to hold it better. A dog has to learn how to carry a dummy and then, as part of the natural progression, to carry game. To do this, it is a good idea to vary the weight and type of dummy during the learning stage. Occasionally, some dogs will carry a commercial dummy by the throwing toggle. If your dog does this, cut the toggle off and stick the flap to the side of the dummy so that it has to be carried by the main body.

Walking away as the dog returns, hiding behind trees or other barriers, crouching or even sitting down, can encourage him to return more quickly. Whistling and encouraging the dog verbally may help, but can also sometimes cause him concern – again, you must read the reactions. A dog who walks around you with the dummy can be discouraged from doing so if you stand in front of a

To speed up a return and improve delivery . . .

. . . hiding behind a hedge can help.

wall or fence, so that he cannot go behind you. Also, the dog may be more keen to come directly to you if he sees a gap between your legs that he can head for. Standing with your legs slightly apart can encourage the dog to come right up to you, heading for the gap, where with voice and hands you can slow him down and control his actions. Crouching down and even sitting on the floor also encourages a dog to come closer to you. I regularly use a familiar place to sit and be with my young dogs – an old fallen tree trunk, a wall or a bench seat – and it is surprising how much more confident they are at bringing a retrieve to that place which they associate with praise and pleasure.

Too many times the fear that the dog will run past with the dummy or drop it, prompts trainers to grab for it so that this does not happen. This usually only makes matters worse. Dogs will either drop the dummy farther away or dance out of range of your grasping hand. Do not be in too much of a hurry to take the dummy: let the dog hold it and praise him by rubbing his chest and under the chin. If your dog sits naturally with the dummy, that is good, but if he stands, wait until the habit of holding and delivering is well and truly ingrained before moving on to the sit and deliver. The dog who drops the dummy short can sometimes be encouraged to bring it alongside you and walk to heel carrying it, provided he enjoys carrying it. With the dog walking to heel, you can slow down your pace and, praising him again, gently reach down and rub his chest, waiting a while before taking the dummy. If your dog drops the dummy, allow him to pick it up again before taking it; if he will not pick up the dummy, pick it up yourself but do not make a drama out of it and certainly do not praise.

Make a gap between your legs and encourage the dog up to you.

With a dog who might drop the dummy short, walk along with him at heel.

If you can find some object that the dog will carry without dropping, use that for the retrieves until the holding habit has been instilled. I have often found that a pair of rolled-up woollen gloves, socks or a peaked cap are far more interesting to a dog, perhaps because they smell of the boss. Woollen objects seem to be easy to carry and, although bulky, are light and soft on the mouth. Once you have got the dog regularly and reliably picking it up and bringing it to you, tie that object to a dummy or wrap the dummy in it and use that for the retrieves before using the dummy on its own again.

The other technique I use for dogs who are poor at delivery and run either too fast at you or past you depends on their sitting to the whistle and holding on to the dummy. When the dog is returning and about ten metres away from your position, blow the single blast 'Stop' whistle, gently at first and then building up as though it were a brake. If the 'Stop' whistle has been correctly learnt, this command will take priority over any other action or thought and will bring the dog to a stop in front of you. Rub the chest and praise. If the 'Stop' whistle has not been fully learnt, I often find that a warning 'growl' as the dog is thinking of running past you can also work, followed by calling him to you, but this again depends upon him wanting to hold the dummy as it is easy to frighten him and make him drop it. If he does drop the dummy, do not persevere with the lesson that caused it.

Although not essential, a sitting delivery and a good finish looks right, but too many trainers cause problems by trying to achieve it with force when the dog has a dummy in his mouth. Shouting 'Sit', forcing the dog's rear to the floor and

Either make him sit or gently reach down while he is alongside you.

Carefully take the retrieve without grabbing.

expecting him to hold on to the dummy at the same time can be rather ambitious. If the dog does hold on to the dummy, he may begin to grip it tightly, in anticipation of your aggressive action. If your dog holds the dummy and delivers it to hand, once on the whistle a gentle 'Sit' whistle blow can get the desired result quite easily. Otherwise, put your hand on the rear of the dog and gently guide it to the floor, while rubbing his chest and under his chin. Trying to do too many things at once can confuse the dog, which in turn irritates you. This irritation is transferred to the dog, and if you had a few problems before, they will now multiply.

If, in the final analysis, you cannot get your dog to hold the dummy for the delivery, the following technique may be of help. If your dog will take an object from your hands, give it to him with the command 'Hold'. Let him hold the dummy for a short period and then take it from the mouth with the command 'Dead'. If the dog lets go of the dummy before you get hold of it say 'No' and give it back to the dog again, saying 'Hold' and praising. If you can stroke the dog's chest while he is holding the dummy and gradually work your hand up to hold the dummy, do so. Say 'Dead' and, once the dummy is released, praise the dog again. If your dog will not hold the dummy, gently open his mouth and roll the dummy behind the canine teeth; hold the dummy there and the mouth over it, saying 'Hold' and praising. Do this for only a few seconds and then take the dummy with the 'Dead' command and praise. Gradually build up the period for which the dog will hold the dummy before being given the 'Dead' command to let go.

Once you have the dog holding the dummy you then have the problem of getting him to come up to you with it.

It does not automatically follow that because the dog will hold the dummy while he is sitting or standing, he will carry it to you and hold it in a delivery. Put your dog on the lead and get him to hold the dummy and walk with it. Occasionally stop and take it from the dog, saying 'Dead'. With your dog on the lead, stop, make him sit and hold the dummy and then call him to you. If he comes to you carrying the dummy, give lots of praise; if he drops the dummy before coming up to you, put it in his mouth saying 'Hold', and try once more. Repeating and building up these exercises in short training sessions each day over a number of days, sometimes weeks, should get the desired result.

I must emphasize, however, that this training session is fraught with danger and should be, in my opinion, a last resort. The main danger is that you will try to do too much too quickly and, if unsuccessful, become impatient – which can make the problem almost impossible for you to solve yourself.

With any problem created through your loss of temper, be aware that the dog will relate that unfair punishment to a particular exercise, and often to a particular place. In this case, it is necessary to lay off training for a while and rebuild the relationship which may have suffered. Take a rest from training and, when you restart, do different exercises; approach the problem with a different solution in mind and move to a new training area.

What appears to be a simple operation – sitting with a dummy in the mouth, held high for your taking – is quite a complex series of movements and thoughts. Take each stage step by step and do not at any time lose your cool, otherwise you are bound to take more steps backward than you have taken forward.

DEVELOPING HUNTING

Most dogs are natural hunters. Some will stick at the job, not giving up until they are successful and the game found or flushed; others lack confidence and may return to you quickly after a brief look around. A quality that is valued in any gundog is that of 'sticking his ground' when he has found scent. To see a dog who touches scent and then works that area, exploiting and exploring every piece of ground where he 'reads a story', is a joy. When such a dog moves away from a 'hot' area without a find, you can expect the game to have moved, and if it was shot to have been a runner. In training, we do not want a dog to dwell on an area where there is nothing to be found, and so we encourage him away from there. Out on a retrieve, it is so easy to want to help the dog that you begin to stop him and give directions much too quickly. This encourages him to depend totally on you for the find, and does not prompt him to learn by experience how to read and work scent. In doing both of these things, it is easy to develop this wide, even patternless, hunting in a dog, where he does not believe his own nose and is constantly looking to you to find the retrieve for him.

There needs to be a balance between initiative and control. Once directed into an area by the handler, the dog should bring to bear his own skills and natural abilities. In the early stages of training, the dog should be encouraged to hunt, even if he covers a much larger area than you will finally accept. Tennis balls in long grass and other cover can be very useful for developing hunting ability. Pushing the ball under a grass sod or hiding it either in straw or in a pile of grass will weaken the scent and get the dog working harder with his nose. Help him to succeed by encouraging him to hunt in the right area but do not direct him to the exact spot. Very few Guns know exactly where a bird has dropped, but they do know the approximate area. A hunting dog will succeed in these situations where a dog who just responds to handling can fail.

In tests, judges can tell you exactly where a dummy is placed – it is in the same position for each dog – and by handling, you can put the dog right on to the dummy; but in a trial, as in the shooting field, you will only be told the area in which the bird required has fallen. In all retrieving exercises, work at developing your dog's hunting ability and at keeping him within the productive areas, but also learn to read when your dog is on scent and is moving away from what you considered to be a productive area because that is where the scent is taking him. Also become familiar with the movements of your dog that show he is not on to anything in particular and is just running or, worse, has lost interest. Your skills as a handler can then come to the fore – encouraging, commanding, helping or just leaving alone.

By laying a line, where a dummy or dead game is dragged on the end of a long piece of twine, and a retrieve placed at the end of the drag, the dog can be sent to the start of the drag and, through experience and encouragement, taught to follow the scent trail. Initially, do not lay too long a trail: the dog should find the dummy at the end of a short tracking of the scent – start with quick success to build confidence. The length of the drag can be increased and, once the dog is regularly succeeding on his own, occasionally throw the retrieve a short distance from where the drag ended. The dog will then learn to cast around a short distance from where he lost the scent, in an attempt to pick it up again. Some birds may give off little scent before they tuck into cover, others can flip into the air or flap a short distance over an obstacle such as a ditch before again tucking into cover or dying. This exercise will help prepare the dog for such occurrences.

If you are training a retriever, there is no reason why you should not hunt him as you would a spaniel. Encouraging the dog to hunt for a hidden dummy by quartering his ground will develop a hunting pattern that helps him make good his ground and not miss game. You will also find that on many shoots, most of your time picking up is spent sweeping – quartering the ground with your dogs looking for birds that might be there, although no one knows exactly where. Endeavour to plant dummies or dead game when the dog is not looking; otherwise he will learn that you are going to be dropping dummies and will watch you rather than hunt. Dogs become very clever at reading your every move. Your hand moves towards the dummy bag and the dog stops to watch knowing that a dummy is coming. Even the sound of a dummy falling is enough to teach the dog to watch you, so plant dummies carefully, otherwise the exercise can be valueless.

Spaniel Hunting

The spaniel has a powerful hunting instinct. Bred with the aim of producing a dog to quest for and to find game, hunting is his main function in life. With some spaniels this hunting instinct is very strong and, coupled with a natural working pattern, makes the training very straightforward. However, some dogs do have to be taught to hunt a pattern, with the use of the whistle, and planted dummies which they find at strategic points in a hunting exercise. With some spaniels, the hunting instinct is quite withdrawn, and there is a need to 'get the dog going' to bring out the hunting ability. I do sometimes find that trainers stifle their dog's inclination to hunt mainly because they are afraid that they will get away from them and run wild. If you have created the right relationship and control this is not usually the case and, even if the dog begins to chase, you should be able to put it right once the dog has learnt what life and his job is all about.

If a dog is not hunting with enthusiasm it is worth introducing him to the smell of the real thing in the rabbit pen or on land where there is a small amount of game. If your dog has been over-controlled he will probably be quite sticky to start with, but if you allow him to chase a little, he should soon overcome this and begin to hunt more freely. One or two visits to the rabbit pen and a little enthusiastic hunting can produce a more flowing dog, but be careful not to panic and be too harsh when you do decide to stop him on the flush. If you have instilled the 'Stop' whistle habit well, it should be quite easy to get him into the habit of stopping and then sitting at the point of flush. The skill comes in your reading the situation, and particularly the dog's actions, to know exactly when to blow the 'Stop' whistle.

Handling too harshly at this stage can result in a dog who becomes confused. His instincts tell him to hunt and flush, which you are constantly encouraging, but if he chases at all, he gets punished. With patience and consistency in your action, using hand, whistle and voice, your dog will begin to sit promptly on the flush. Once the dog knows he is expected to sit promptly, you can administer punishment to fit the crime when he does not. If you shoot any game over your dog during the early stages, pick most of it yourself and, if you send the dog for a retrieve, make him wait before sending him. A good rule is to break your gun and reload before sending the dog – but keep an eye on him! A retrieve is the fulfilment of the hunt and the kill, but your dog must not expect to fetch the game every time, otherwise he will begin to run in. I know of some beaters who will not allow their dogs to retrieve any game shot during a drive, so that the habit is not allowed to establish itself in any way.

Your spaniel will have to hunt a variety of countryside and learn how to find and work scent. If you continually hunt your spaniel where there is no game, he will begin to lose interest; some spaniels need more game than others to maintain their enthusiasm. Where game is easily seen, a spaniel can develop the habit of looking, and even staring, rather than hunting with his nose. The ideal, therefore, is ground which has cover that the dog has to investigate but which contains enough game to keep him interested. By running your dog over ground which does not hold game, firing shots and throwing dummies which he then retrieves, you will end up with a dog who runs in a questing pattern but is not hunting. He will wait for you to fire and throw. Some dogs who are frequently run in tests end up like this; they become what is termed test wise.

As scent can be at varying heights from the ground, your dog must learn how to find the scent in varying cover. In root crops, such as stubble turnip, fodder beet

Give your dog experience of hunting a wide variety of cover and terrain such as ditches and reeds.

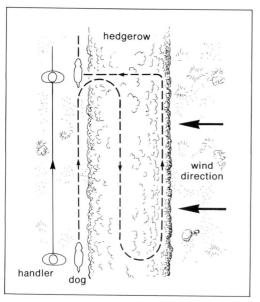

Fig 1

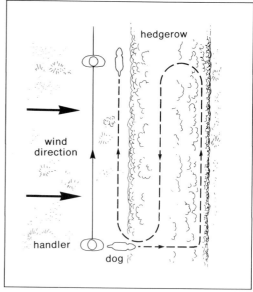

Fig 2

Figs 1–4   Ideal hunting patterns which will not be achieved perfectly.
In practice, if the dog uses the wind – and therefore scent – correctly,
he will work in a similar though not symmetrical pattern. To control
the hunting, call the dog back to you regularly so that he is taking
'bites' at the hunting pattern. This means double-hunting the ground
in places but it will keep him within shooting distance.

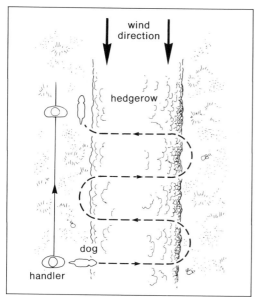

Fig 3

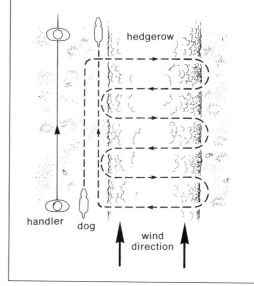

Fig 4

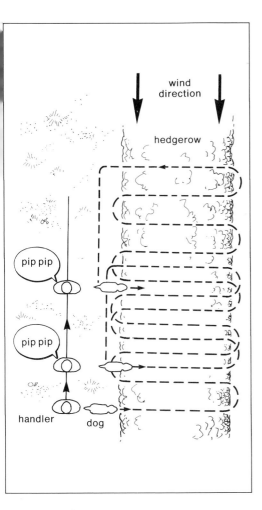

wind
direction

hedgerow

pip pip

pip pip

handler   dog

Fig 5   Double hunting in practice.

One of the special qualities of a spaniel is his optimism, and he really comes into his own when game is scarce and the job is to find that elusive rabbit or bird for the gun. To do this the dog will have to learn to hunt ditches, hedgerows, riverbanks and other difficult ground in addition to woodland fields of a variety of crops. When you approach difficult hunting ground, think through the best method of approaching it. What is the wind direction? How can you give the dog the advantage regarding scent while also maintaining contact and control over him? Are there places where your dog will be out of sight and could this cause a problem? Overgrown ditches and hedgerows are particularly problematical and a dog can easily run a considerable distance, and even chase game, when he is out of your sight under cover, or on the blind side of a hedge.

With young dogs who are inexperienced, I do not allow them to be out of sight for longer than a few seconds: I want them to be checking that I am still there and, in doing so, I know where they are. With older dogs whom you know and whose habits are good, you can relax a little, but with any dog you should concentrate, watch and listen. In certain cover, you can work the dog by sound and movement within that cover. The intensity of rustling, the difference in sound between your dog and a bird or rabbit, and the wing noise as a bird is attempting to take off through the cover, are all noises that you should recognize, helping you manage the situation and carry out the appropriate actions.

In hedgerows, if the wind is blowing from your side through the hedge, the dog must learn to go to the far side of the hedge as well as to work up the middle. With dry ditches, the dog must learn to

or sugar beet, the dog should be getting his nose under the leaves to find the scent. Too often, an inexperienced dog will be seen bouncing among the crop like a small deer and not getting down to the job. It is a pleasure to watch a dog who knows his business when he comes to scent: one minute the nose is on the ground taking a foot scent, the next it is higher to take a level of air scent. Through experience, he begins to read the messages and knows how to locate the game.

get down into the bottom of the ditch and not to keep jumping across it to hunt either bank. With help and guidance, your dog will quickly gain the necessary experience to deal with varied and difficult terrain.

Bracken which has died down forms a carpet which harbours game, and your dog must learn to get under this carpet to find and flush. Bouncing over the top of dead bracken can frighten game but in many cases the game will tuck in and sit tight. Encourage your dog to investigate under this cover by lifting it with your hand and showing him holes and weaknesses in it where he can enter. After a while, most dogs find this type of cover not only interesting but fun, entering it low down and then bursting through it. If game is found, this becomes even more fun and, once they have learnt that the

cover will produce what their heart desires if attacked correctly, the habit becomes natural. When developing this bracken hunting, start with bracken that is not too flat to the ground and is not growing around very spindly bramble. Flat, brambly bracken is very restricting, difficult and uncomfortable for an inexperienced dog to hunt; a young dog can be put off by it and learn to run around it, not entering correctly, and only sniffing at strategic points. To do the job properly, the cover needs to be entered and taken apart, so if you start with easier types of cover and build up to the more difficult as the enthusiasm of the dog increases, the problems are minimized.

To work behind a hard-hunting spaniel with style and drive is, for me, the most exhilarating part of dog work. The antici-

Give a clear decisive cast-off when you start your dog, 'Seek on'.

pation of a flush and a shot, coupled with the pleasure of watching a questing dog who will communicate with me through his actions, make a day with a good spaniel one to be totally enjoyed. Always be aware, however, that those natural instincts which create so much pleasure when channelled and controlled, can also be the ruination of a shooting day if uncontrolled.

ADVANCED WATER WORK

Advanced water work should not be attempted until you have mastered advanced exercises on land. It must be realized that on land, if the dog does anything wrong, you can get out to him and help put him right; on water, that poss-

ibility is minimized. Therefore, to lessen the risk of problems occurring, you must be confident that you can handle advanced situations on dry land.

Distance retrieves and multiple retrieves; distractions, with dummies being thrown while the dog is on his way to a prior retrieve or on his way back with dummy in mouth; retrieves across a large stretch of water and on to land; and multiple retrieves on land and water are all exercises that your dog should be capable of carrying out. Initially, start these exercises on stretches of water where there are no currents and the wind is not blowing hard enough to push the dummies away from the fall area. Once the dog is confident in still water, you can gradually introduce currents and sea water, but take it gently as this can be

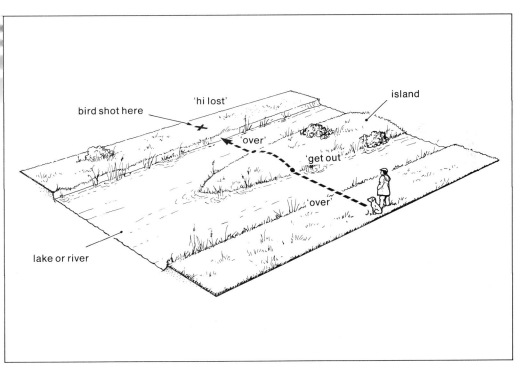

Fig 6   Retrieve over an island.

Stand back from the edge of the water. The dog should not shake until he has delivered the bird.

Once he has completed he retrieve, the dog can get rid of all the excess water.

A good, bold entry always looks exciting but be careful to ensure that there is little possibility of underwater obstruction to hurt the dog.

unnerving to some dogs. You should practise sending your dog for seen and unseen retrieves, standing at increasing distances from the edge of the water, ensuring that when he returns, he brings the dummy all the way back without dropping it or shaking himself. Develop the dog's ability to cross two stretches of water to reach a retrieve. There are times when a bird will fall across two stretches of water, or there is an island in the middle of a lake which the dog will have to cross on his way to the retrieve. As you can imagine, this is not the easiest retrieve: the dog will often think that the bird is on the first land he reaches and it is then a difficult job to push him across another stretch of water.

To get your dog over rivers and stretches of water it will help if he understands that when you say 'Over', it means get over an obstacle whether this be a fence or water. By understanding what you require when you say 'Over', the dog will look further than the obstacle he is faced with and know that the retrieve is on the other side. Situations where the retrieve has not been seen or where the river bank cannot be seen by you can be made less difficult if the dog will obey this command. Where the river's edge is below a steep bank, your dog will go out of sight and, with many dogs, this results in their hunting the nearside bank where you are out of contact. By giving the command 'Over' as you send him, and then possibly repeating it once more as he reaches the top of the bank and is going out of sight, there is a greater chance of success (provided the dog has been taught the command).

Reeds and waterside bushes or other cover can also cause problems with a dog who loves to hunt cover, and you must be able to push him out from this cover when the situation demands it. To train

Teach your dog to take directions on the opposite bank of a river or lake.

When he reaches the opposite bank, make him stop and then give a clear signal.

your dog to go over water and handle bankside cover, start with narrow streams and rivers where you can be nearer to the dog as he attempts these exercises. This closeness gives you more control and, if it is a stream which you can cross, you can still get out to the dog and help overcome any problems that arise. After crossing rivers or lakes, many dogs will shake as they emerge. This is acceptable on the way out to a dummy, and if you know your dog does this, give him the time to do so before taking control once more and continuing with the directions. Ducks and even pheasants can tuck into reeds and the swampy edge of river margins, and these birds often take some finding. You must give your dog the experience which will enable him to know what you want him to do – hunt the edge or go away from the river on the opposite side.

Although I rarely use a dummy launcher, it can prove very useful where the rivers are wide and you need to propel a dummy well over. If there is a bridge (for your own use), close enough for you to run over and get in contact with the dog, should the need arise, this can be a great help. The problem here is that, without intending to, you can teach the dog to look for bridges rather than swimming directly out and back. In a test, I would not penalize a dog for returning via a bridge, or by land around a lake, provided it was easy to do so – the game would be brought back more quickly and there is less likelihood of its being damaged. However, I would not think so well of a dog who went running up and down the far bank looking for an easier way when one was not available, or running a considerable distance to avoid swimming.

Once you have got a dog working in water, he often tends to handle better than on land. This may be because there are fewer distractions and also because he is not able to move so fast, however excited he is. I have seen long check cords used on a dog in water to stop him making for the far bank and to guide him back to the handler once he has a retrieve. Such an aid is not easy to use, and you have to be careful not to let the dog or objects in or around the water get entangled. This could cause more panic and resultant problems than you had to start with.

As with working on land, the more experience your dog has on water, the more he will learn and the more accomplished he will become, but do take it in easy stages: if you are too ambitious and you get into difficulty, it is not easy to correct or help the dog when he is in the middle of a lake. This causes frustration, and even anger, on the part of the handler, which only makes matters worse. The majority of dogs I have known have not only enjoyed water but really looked forward to swimming. However, good lessons can be quickly unlearnt when water is involved: dogs who are steady on land can run in when the retrieve is on water; a dog who stops on the whistle may ignore you and swim in circles, looking for the retrieve, rather than looking to you for support. Of course, you do not expect the dog to stop and sit in water, but he should look to you for the command which will follow the whistle blast. For these reasons, your dog must have a sound grounding in basics and advanced training on land before progressing to advanced training on water.

Remember, swimming during water training is very tiring, and your dog will be using his muscles in a different way, which can cause stiffness and pain. So do not overdo it. One problem that is quite common is a physical injury some people

Encourage a clean, positive exit with the retrieve. The dog should not drop the bird.

call lamb's tail: after water work, the dog's tail actually droops through loss of vitality caused by physical stress during the work. It usually disappears after a day or two and as your dog builds up his swimming muscles, it should not happen at all. However, some dogs do get it throughout their working life.

Not only will experience and training on water be of value on shooting days but, also, many gundog associations run water tests which demand that the dog completes exercises incorporating advanced work. Should you also be interested in field trials, water work is an essential feature of making a dog into a Field Trial Champion and your dog must have proved that he will enter and retrieve from water. In the Retriever and Spaniel Championships, all dogs who qualify for awards must have completed a water retrieve in the competition, and these

retrieves are not always easy or straightforward.

CREATING SITUATIONS

As your dog develops, and is able to perform the basic and advanced exercises successfully, it becomes necessary to stretch both his ability and your own to handle those difficult situations that you will encounter in the field. If you are familiar with the shooting field, you can use this experience to devise exercises that simulate what could happen. There are a multitude of different situations that you can construct: dead birds, runners, differing cover, more than one bird down, water. And different types of shooting: walking up and driven or rough shooting where you shoot over a questing dog. If you do not know much

Give your dog experience of retrieving through hedges.

Initially, natural gaps will help him to succeed.

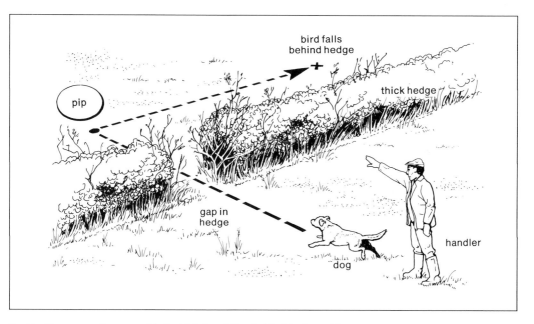

Fig 7 Unseen retrieve on a bird which has fallen behind hedge with a gap. The dog is kept in view and then directed right where he has to work on his own initiative out of sight.

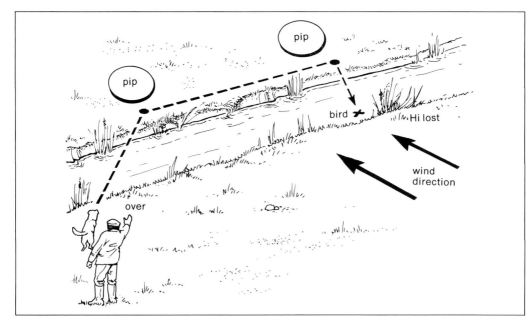

Fig 8   Unseen retrieve on bird in stream or ditch.

about shooting and what can happen in the field, it is worth attending a training class or seeking out a knowledgeable dog trainer. Always ask, when an exercise is set, what situation is being simulated so that you can get an understanding of what could happen and therefore be prepared if you ever come up against it. Where practical, runners should always be collected before dead birds, so if you put out a number of dummies for your dog, decide the order in which you want them picked up, and work at getting the dog to retrieve in that order.

Multiple retrieves are common for the Gun's dog and the picking-up dog. It is a great advantage if the dog is able to remember more than one bird down and to pick them in the order you require them. Build up the number of dummies thrown – six is usually thought to be the maximum number your dog will remember. Start with a split retrieve – two

dummies. A clear, decisive signal should be used to send the dog for the dummy you require him to pick. He will initially want to pick the last one you threw but if you position the dog in the direction of the dummy you require first and if that dummy is closer, even in view, so that he can find it quickly, he will begin to learn to take your 'casting off' directions. It is also a good idea to say 'No' when you throw the dummy you do not want retrieved first.

When you move on to three and more dummies the word 'No' can be used while pointing in their direction, prior to positioning the dog for the dummy you do require. Your dog must be completely steady at this stage and not run-in to the pointing of the arm. If you have done the basics correctly, he should only move when you say 'Fetch it' or 'Get Out' together with the arm signal. One top trainer goes even further: he says the dog's name, touches the side of his face and then gives the command to retrieve. The dog should not move unless all three signals have been given. Saying the name of the dog prior to any command is useful when you are running more than one dog, or when other handlers and dogs are working close to you and their commands could easily cause a reaction in your dog. Your dog only obeys when he hears his name prior to the command.

Unseen retrieves can be placed at various distances and in places where their location could prove difficult. Gateways, hollows in the ground, bases of trees and walls or fences, and cover that holds the retrieve off the ground (even if only a foot) can cause all kinds of problems which you and your dog must be able to deal with. Unseen retrieves can be used alongside seen retrieves, where a dog is told to ignore the seen retrieve and fetch an unseen first. In the shooting field, this is often necessary where the dog has marked the fall of a dead bird but the runner, which you want first, was not marked. The dog has to ignore the dead bird and hunt in the direction of the runner, believing that there is something there to find. This is the secret of unseen retrieves – the dog has to trust you and believe that with your help he will find that retrieve.

To develop your dog's trust, put down an unseen only a short distance from where he will be sent, and at a wide angle to the dummy which you will throw for the dog to see. Once the dummy has been thrown, say 'No' to the dog, turn him in the direction of the unseen and, with a clear signal and verbal command 'Get Out', send him in the direction of the unseen. If it is only a short distance away, your dog should succeed quite easily in finding it, par-

ticularly if you have used paths or hedgerows to guide him. Should the dog try to avoid you and go for the seen retrieve, stop him immediately, bring him back to the starting point and send him once more for the unseen, helping him if necessary by walking towards the unseen. Once successful, the dog should be praised. Distances and the number of unseens can be increased as your dog builds confidence. If you have only practised with single unseen retrieves so far, you may find that, once the dog has done one retrieve, he does not always show enthusiasm for another one – he thinks he has completed the job.

At any time during a retrieving exercise, you should be able to recall your dog to your side. This may be necessitated by other dogs picking up the bird you were after, the bird taking off and flying away or a dangerous situation suddenly occurring. Wounded birds can run across roads or over electrified railway lines, and they can be washed away on a strong tide into heavy seas. In my mind, no retrieve is worth the life of my dog – if you can stop him and recall him, you could save a lot of unhappiness. To teach your dog immediate recall, sit the dog away from you and throw the dummy over his head. Recall the dog to your side before sending him for the retrieve or picking it up yourself. Occasionally send the dog for a retrieve and then stop and recall him before he reaches the dummy, perhaps sending him for a different one. This exercise has another value in that it will prepare your dog for those occasions when he is out on a retrieve for a dead bird and another is shot and wounded, a potential runner. If you can stop your dog and redirect him on to the wounded bird immediately, it is less likely to escape; once successful, you

Get the dog accustomed to distraction on the way out and on the return. Here, a dummy is being thrown as the dog returns with his retreive. The moment the dummy is launched, encourage your dog up to you with the dummy he is already carrying.

can then turn your dog's attention back to the dead bird retrieve. This stopping, recalling and redirecting has to be done carefully and in moderation, otherwise your dog may become sticky – running out a short distance before stopping and looking back to ask 'Are you going to change your mind?'

In the shooting field, there will be many distractions, tempting your dog to do the wrong thing and taking his mind off the task in hand. Guns firing, birds and rabbits flushing, game being shot, and other dogs, are only some of the distractions he will have to cope with. Your dog must learn to stick to the job in hand; he must recognize the difference between the blood scent of a wounded or dead animal and the scent of an unshot one (this will mostly come from experience). But you can use extra dummies and shots to simulate other birds being

shot while he is going out on a retrieve and when he is returning with a retrieve in his mouth. If your dog is returning with a retrieve and you throw another dummy which he can see, he must bring you the one in his mouth first: if the dummy in his mouth was a wounded but strong runner and he let go of it to fetch a second, it does not take a lot of imagination to envisage the problems that would be caused. Any retrieve in the mouth of the dog must be brought directly to you before he is sent for another.

When first starting this exercise, throw the second dummy behind you so that the dog can see it as he is returning with the first. If he is tempted, he will have to get past you in order to reach the second dummy, and in this position you can block his path. Encourage the dog up to you and take the delivery, then make him

Work with others to create situations. At this training class, dogs at the rear are being sent through others for retrieves.

wait while you pick the second dummy yourself. When you can do this successfully, without the dog being tempted to fetch the second dummy, throw the dummy out to the side as he returns and be very prompt in calling him up if he falters. In time, you should be able to throw the second dummy anywhere, even over the dog's head or in front of his nose; and he should totally ignore its existence unless you give the 'Fetch' command.

Some dogs become very clever at this exercise and, on the way back, stop and mark the fall of the second dummy. This really is a plus point as they can then quickly retrieve the second bird and put it in the bag. One of my older dogs became so adept at this in demonstrations at game fairs that on his return, instead of facing me with the retrieve, he would turn to face the dummy I had thrown as a distraction. If I backed away, he would come neatly up to me and then promptly turn around before sitting to face the distraction dummy. He never dropped the first dummy and he only did this in demonstrations, which, although not a textbook performance, created a very amusing and entertaining piece of comedy for the audience. He had become demonstration-wise!

In your training sessions try to set up situations that you will encounter in the field and, if you have encountered problems on shooting days, devise ways of simulating them in order to give the dog experience and training which will minimize these difficulties in the future.

3 Days in the Field – the Real Thing

GETTING THE WORK

Although some trainers stop at dummy work and are quite content to make tests their final objective, most dog trainers use dummies and tests as a stepping stone to the real work of a gundog – working in the field on game and other live quarry. The problem is that, if you do not have a shoot of your own, it may be very difficult to get the work for you and your dog. Whoever said 'it's not what you know but who you know' was right: there is no quicker way into the field than by knowing the right people. If you do not already know the right people, you have to put yourself in a position where you can meet them. Invitations to a shoot are not automatic, and you and your dog will have to prove yourselves if you are to be asked or recommended.

A shoot involves a lot of people, and its success depends on them all doing their own particular job well. As with all team jobs, it may only take a small mistake by one member to mess it all up. Members of a shoot are therefore very careful about who they invite, and if you are invited you can expect a wary eye to be kept on you in the early days, particularly by the keeper. This is not to say that shoots are not friendly events – they are and full of good humour, but they will not suffer fools or poor workers.

There are a number of ways to make the right contacts. One of the most useful is to join a gundog training club or a shooting club such as a wildfowler's association. The British Association for Shooting and Conservation at Marford Mill will give you the name of your nearest wildfowling club. By their very nature, these clubs consist of people who have an interest and participate in shooting. Some clubs even offer a beating and picking-up team to the local shoots or are asked by the local shoots if they can find interested dog people to work for them. Shoot owners and keepers are placing their reputation and hard work in the hands of a beater or picker-up, and they are more likely to feel comfortable in doing this if they feel that the dog and handler has been well trained. A club gives them more assurance that this is the case. Many keepers and shoot owners themselves are very interested in dog work, taking an active part in clubs and competitions, or offering their ground for club events. If they see you and your dog performing well, an invitation can quite easily follow.

Join a club that is involved in advancing the working ability of your chosen breed. There are specialist breed clubs, but there are also clubs that cater for a wide variety of gundog breeds. If you are unsure about the clubs in your area, the Kennel Club in Clarges Street, London will be able to give you the names of

ffiliated clubs and the secretary to con-
act for membership and information.

If you have friends who work their
dogs on a shoot, they may be able to get
an invitation for you. Initially, it may
only be an occasional invitation to fill in
for a regular shoot member who cannot
be there on that particular day. If you do
your job well, however, and it is noticed
by the keeper, you may find yourself
becoming one of the regulars. One of the
main problems you will come up against
is that shoots are not held only on Satur-
days; in fact, the majority are run on a
week day, which means that you have to
be free during the week or willing to take
the day as a holiday from work. If you are
able to attend a shoot on weekdays, you
will probably find it easier to get the
work. More people can attend on Satur-
days than on weekdays.

As there are more beaters than pickers-
up required on a shoot, beating work is
easier to obtain. Beating is a way into a
shoot, but once you have gained experience and demonstrated that you have a
controllable dog, you may then be asked
to pick-up. Of course, it may be that you
have a hunting dog, such as a spaniel, and
beating is of most interest to you. There is
no doubt that a good spaniel in the beating
line is worth a handful of human beaters.
The emphasis is on 'good', and because
this standard has been found to be a
rarity, a few shoots will not allow dogs in
the beating line. So check on this before
you offer your services, if you want to
work your dog.

Keenness and a willingness to work for
the shoot and the keeper will reap its
rewards. Once you have made the contacts and you have their confidence, offer
to 'dog in' the boundaries (stopping the
birds from wandering off the shoot), or
ask whether they would like your help

cold picking the next morning (looking
for birds that could have been missed or
were wounded and died in the night,
often dropping from the trees where they
roosted).

Keepering is a hard job with long
hours, and reliable, trustworthy help is
valued. Your reward will not only be the
thanks and respect of the keeper, but also
the opportunity to work with and train
your dog to a higher standard.

FITNESS FOR WORK

Working your dog in the field requires a
high degree of fitness and stamina on
your part, and more on the part of your
dog. For every mile you walk, a spaniel
quartering the ground in front of you
will probably cover five or more, and
through much thicker cover. Can you
imagine the energy that goes into driving
your body through thick brambles and
undergrowth or keeping up the pace on
heavy boggy ground thick with rushes?
This is what your dog is faced with, and
if you have not prepared him for this
commando course, he will not last the
day and may suffer injury.

Some grounds are more demanding
than others: steep hills, heavy undergrowth and soil that builds up on your
boots can be very tiring, as can the
grouse moors where you have to walk
miles over very difficult terrain and, in
August or September, very warm weather.
How you get yourself fit is up to you, but
you have a responsibility to your dog to
make sure that he can stand the rigours of
a shoot day. A dog is not like a gun, which
can be laid up during the summer months
and then taken out and put into action at
the beginning of the season. If you are a
keen trainer, you have probably been

working with dummies throughout the summer months. A short training session, however, is not the same as a full day's shooting. Most dogs, given the opportunity and the correct diet, will keep themselves fit, but I particularly feel for the spaniel who has spent the summer months relaxing around the house and then, with no preparation, is expected to spend a full day beating.

Dogging in the boundaries, spells of hunting thick cover and swimming will help to revitalize and tone up the working muscles. For the retriever, long memory retrieves (where you drop the dummy and walk on with the dog for increasing distances before sending him back for it) will help to stretch the legs. Remember, also, that as the body tires so, too, does the brain. In fact, I believe that the brain tires more quickly than the body and, although a dog may still be going with some pace, he could be exhausted mentally. Even with the experienced campaigner, it is worth carrying out training exercises, even some of the basic ones, to refine, tone up and remind the dog of what is required.

If you have more than one dog, you may decide not to work them both for the whole day, preferring to work each for short periods interspersed with rests. Fitness is still important, even in this situation, if your dog is to give his best and concentrate on the job at hand. Two or more dogs will help to keep themselves fit by running around with each other. During the summer evenings a walk along the seafront, where it is allowed, letting the dogs run through the water and swim in the sea will help to tone and strengthen the muscles. This is useful exercise for wildfowling dogs who may have to deal with water in order to reach a retrieve.

It is surprising how a dog who may be accustomed to short bursts of activity followed by long periods of rest, learns to pace himself when he reaches the shooting field. On the first few outings, he will usually put everything into his first half-hour of work, but, after a few weeks of working, realize that he is there for the day and begin to work in a lower gear until there is a need for a burst of high energy. This is the reason that some field triallers do not work their dogs for long periods: they do not want them to pace themselves for a long period of work, but to give maximum output for the short period that they are under the scrutiny of a judge, to achieve maximum concentration and eye-catching performance.

COUNTRYSIDE ETIQUETTE

It is a sad fact of life that today many people adopt the attitude that they can do and say what they like and, if others do not care for it, that is their hard luck. The shooting world, country sports and related gundog work are full of traditions and etiquette. Politeness and a respect for other people's property and feelings should be the norm, and etiquette is founded on this. Traditions and behaviour particular to shooting are part of the total enjoyment of the sport and a great part of our history. Society is changing and there have been many changes in the shooting field, but the pleasure of the sport and of working dogs can be enhanced by observing the ways which are accepted and respected by all.

I have mentioned some of the 'do's' and 'don'ts' particular to certain types of work in the sections of the book, but there are one or two points that are worthy of mention here.

If your dog is not up to the required standard for work in the field, then do ot offer your services: you could be an embarrassment to the keeper as well as to yourself, and will probably never get asked again. It may be worth asking more experienced dog people their advice if you are not sure what will be expected of you, and whether you and your dog come up to the required standard.

Always be at the meeting place in good time and let the organizers know that you are available. Dress correctly for the occasion. Today, no one expects best shooting suits, but it is presumed that you will dress cleanly and smartly in appropriate clothing. I have seen beaters and pickers-up in some very unsightly apparel: boiler suits, wellington boots with steel toecaps and jackets so old and ragged even the men of the road would refuse them. Dog handlers who are in close proximity to the Guns should make a particular effort to appear in acceptable dress.

Tact, diplomacy and an understanding of human behaviour will hold you in good stead. Arguing or disagreeing with Guns and keepers is not on. Some shoots frown upon dog handlers socializing in any way with the Guns and, though this may seem archaic, it can create a safer environment for all. Whatever you do, do not comment to a Gun on his shooting if it is at a low ebb. This can be extremely irritating and make you most unpopular. If a Gun is behaving in an unsafe manner, move to a safe position and bring the matter to the attention of the keeper – quietly.

Remember the Countryside Code and be particular about closing gates, respecting boundaries and creating as little disturbance as possible around farm livestock. If crossing fences, use a stile where one is provided, or learn how to climb over them without straining the wire and creating damage. Where you are ac-

companying Guns crossing fences or streams, offer to hold their guns while they negotiate the obstacle. Make sure that they are unloaded and broken.

You and your dog should cause minimum nuisance to other members of a shoot and behave in such a way that it enhances the pleasure of their day. There is no doubt that if you do this, you will also gain much more pleasure from the day and will become part of the team.

COUNTRYSIDE DRESS

Choice of dress will depend upon the shooting and dog work you involve yourself in. What is right for one may be totally unacceptable for the other. The pigeon shooter generally favours the broken pattern of camouflage clothing; the picker-up at a formal shoot, a tweed-type jacket and breeks, sometimes with the added formality of shirt and tie; for the wildfowler, layers of warm clothing and waterproof over clothes, plus waders, are required.

Today, there seems to be some items of clothing that are acceptable wherever you are – waxproofed coats and breeks coupled with the well-known green wellingtons. Hats tend to reflect personal taste and, provided that they are tasteful, can be left to your own particular preference. A game bag is always a very useful addition to your kit. Even if you do not require it for game, you can carry your waterproofs for when you may require them, some first aid kit (for yourself and your dog), a sandwich in case your body craves sustenance, and any other paraphernalia to help you through the day.

When deciding what to wear, consider the type of activity as well as the occasion. Standing around waiting prior to picking up can be very cold, whereas working in the beating line can certainly bring out the sweat in you. There are so many different types of clothing on the market to meet every requirement, made of thermal materials, fabrics that breath and waterproof cloth, that you have a wealth of choice. Feeling comfortable, warm and part of the scene will make your day that much more enjoyable.

FIRST AID FOR YOUR DOG

The shooting field is a battle ground for your dog, with many an obstacle to cause injury; such injury is usually minor, but unfortunately sometimes major. One of the worst pieces of farm equipment ever invented for dog work is barbed wire, and a season rarely passes without one of my dogs tearing himself on it.

One of the most vulnerable parts of a spaniel is the point at which the front leg meets the body. The skin here is quite soft and tears easily, leaving either a flap of skin or a large hole where the skin has pulled away from the flesh. I have seen bitches who have had their teats ripped off, and dogs who have had their penises badly cut. It does not matter how careful you are around fences – there is still the hidden wire in the hedgerow waiting for the unsuspecting and enthusiastic dog. Small cuts and punctures can be cleaned and liberally dusted with an anti-bacterial powder. Large wounds may need stitching, in which case clean as well as you can and apply a field dressing. Take the dog to the vet as quickly as possible for stitching. I never cease to be amazed at how a dog can continue to work oblivious to the fact that he has hurt himself quite badly. You may not notice the wound at first because the dog is running through long grass or wet cover and cleaning the blood away.

Puncture wounds under the legs and body are not always found until the end of the day when the dog begins to lick them, or when you are checking him over.

Thorns from brambles catch in the skin and can remain there for days unless the dog is checked over after, or even at a convenient moment during, the shoot. If left in there, the area can become septic; if in the foot, the resulting pain will cause the dog to limp. Blackthorn in particular will cause a very sensitive wound, and it is worth checking the dog over quite carefully if he has been working in cover of this nature. Even grass seeds can puncture the dog's skin, especially between the toes, and work their way into his body. Often this results in a small cyst, which may have to be operated on in order to remove the seed.

Grass seeds, pollen and dust from bushes such as gorse can build up in your dog's eyes, particularly if he has drooping lower lids. Eyes should be wiped out with a damp piece of cotton wool and a couple of eye drops used to ease any discomfort and reduce the chance of future problems. Cut ears, tongues and tails are common and, generally, these look worse than they are, with a lot of blood from a very small wound. Bracken, brambles, reeds and even grasses can cause these and, unless exceptional, they quickly heal.

In the event of your dog being injured in more than a very minor way, always seek the advice and treatment of a vet. In no way can first aid treatment be a substitute for professional help – it is an initial treatment which will ease the suffering of your dog until you can get him to a vet and provide a basis for later care.

The snake bite is another problem that can occur, although in this country only the adder is poisonous. Unless you see your dog being bitten, you may not realize first that this has happened. The symptoms can be quite distressing and the dog may appear to be in a state of collapse. However, the snake bite is not usually fatal, unless in the throat area where the swelling could choke the dog. If your dog should be bitten by a snake, get him to a vet as quickly as possible. In the meantime, an anti-histamine tablet, such as Piriton, can be administered to counteract the effect of the venom, but as soon as you have got him to the vet, tell him what you have done.

Wasp and bee stings can also be uncomfortable and, if around the face area, cause swelling. Be particularly observant of the condition of your dog if he was stung in the mouth or throat, as any swelling here could restrict his breathing.

It is worth while carrying a small first-aid pack around in your game bag as you never know when or where an injury can occur. Some of the most important contents of the pack would be:

a large field dressing
cotton wool and/or lint
eye drops
a roll of elastoplast
scissors
tweezers
Piriton tablets
anti-bacterial powder such as Acrimide

In addition to the first-aid kit, a large towel, a container of fresh water and a drinking bowl will prove invaluable during the day. Many Guns let their dogs drink from any puddle that is around – in fact, it is sometimes difficult to stop them doing so. However, I do know of one dog who drank from a puddle which contained a highly toxic substance which killed him. Regular offerings of fresh water will minimize the chance of this happening.

At the end of any work, it is worth while checking your dog over to ensure that he has not received any injury. Inspect all the vulnerable areas for cuts and tears, run your hands over his body to feel for thorns and deep scratches. Remove thorns and dab the puncture marks and scratches with antiseptic. Do not forget to check between the toes and in the ears for seeds or other irritants. For scratches around the feet, I find that a strong salt and warm water solution in a jam jar, in which the foot is then soaked for a few minutes, works wonders.

Prompt treatment can prevent minor wounds from becoming worse, so that you are not without a dog for longer than you would wish. Look after your dog first, your gun second and then, if you have the energy, yourself.

4 Dogging-In

Once a keeper has reared his pheasants and released them on the shoot ground, one of his prime objectives is to keep them there. Pheasants are not renowned for their intelligence and they have a knack of wandering away from the protection of the coverts and the feed lines. Perhaps they are not so stupid if you consider that we are keeping them there to shoot in the future. When there is a lot of natural food around such as beech mast and acorns or when other farmers on surrounding estates have tempting maize growing, the job of the keeper to hold the birds is very difficult and time consuming. Offers of help to dog-in on the estate are usually well received if you are known and trusted by the keeper and you have a good reputation with dogs.

Working the edges of the estate to push back the birds that are being tempted to leave home ground can be very good training; it is exciting work and also an interesting and rewarding job. If you start doing the work during the early days when the birds have not been long out of the release pen and only a few are attempting to play truant, it is a very useful way to introduce a young dog to live game and the flush.

The advantages to the keeper of having his birds dogged are more than just keeping them in. It will accustom the birds to being driven and moved in a particular direction. The birds will become dog conscious: if they see a dog they will often move back towards the security of their pen or if the dog gets into close contact with them they will learn to fly quite promptly. The dogging and flushing will tend to make them more wild and increase the possibility of their presenting better shots for the Guns. Although it is to the keeper's advantage, you have to realize that he is giving you his trust; he is giving you the run of the estate; and you will know the layout of the pens and the land, and often his routines. This is all useful information to those who would poach his birds. Also, if you do not dog-in correctly, there is the possibility that you will drive the birds away rather than keep them in the required areas.

Make sure that you know the layout of the estate and the weak areas where birds are likely to escape. The keeper will give you instructions and guide-lines but often, when you are out, there will be times when you have to use your own judgement. Get to know which land you can dog back from: some farmers are friendly and will allow this, others have their own shoots and you may be stealing their birds without knowing it. In many cases, the edge of the estate will be alongside a road. Some country-road hedges can be worked quite safely if there is little traffic, your dog is very controllable and you can see the road well ahead and behind. Should you have any doubts at all, walk the dog at heel or put him on a lead and tap the hedgerow out yourself. There is no sense in causing an accident.

When dogging-in with a spaniel, I work him as I would normally, hunting up the boundaries whether they are hedges or ough cover along a fence. At the flush of bird, I sit the dog and make him wait efore giving the command 'Gone Away' nd then hunting on. With retrievers, I walk them to heel, tapping the cover and riving the birds ahead. Where birds may e sitting tight in cover, I will encourage he dog to push them out, spaniel fashion, nd then sit when they flush. With the eeper's permission, I will carry a starting istol and later a shot-gun with blanks once the dog is accustomed to gunfire) nd fire at the departing birds. Occasionlly, I will give the dog a seen or hidden etrieve on a dummy or cold game. If you re the gun in the direction of an unseen hat you have surreptitiously placed down reviously, this will develop your dog's bility to ignore what he has seen and to elieve that he will find something when e goes for an unseen. If possible, where irds are ahead of me and within range, I will throw the retrieve amongst the birds nd send the dog for it. You must have eached a stage where your dog is under lose control and is reliable at retrieving efore doing this. It goes without saying hat you must also have a very undertanding and trusting friend in the keeper.

By working the boundaries regularly nd pushing the birds back, you will egin to know where the most common scape routes are. You will also become amiliar with the number of birds that are o be found wandering. Where there ppears to be an increase in the number of scapees, let the keeper know so that this area can be dogged more regularly. After a while, the birds will get to recognize the dogs and, as soon as they see you coming, return to their own ground. However, you should still work the cover, and the places where birds can tuck in, for the wily ones. The scent will be warm and when a bird is flushed it will be because the dog has had to use his natural ability to find it.

Do keep an eye on your dog while dogging-in as it is easy to do too much with a young dog and get him overexcited. Do a small amount with a young dog and then put him back in the car, continuing with another. If you only have the one dog, put him on a lead or walk him to heel rather than hunt him all the time, to get him into the routine of relaxing and disengaging top gear. The longer the birds have been out of the release pen, the more likely they are to wander, but clever feeding by the keeper and good dog work can prevent a lot of them from straying, and in carrying out this dog work you can be developing your dog's skills ready for the shooting season.

A supportive keeper who recognizes the value of good dogs and encourages their training is worth his weight in gold. He deserves to have the job done well and correctly. Do not dog-in just to train but also to help him – continue with the work even after you have done your training. The benefits will then be realized by both of you.

5 Beating

The aim of beating is to find and work the game towards the waiting line of guns and flush them for the Guns in such a way that they present sporting shots which test their ability. Although it sounds straightforward, there is an art to beating, and a good dog can be a tremendous asset worth a number of human beaters, but a bad dog can be disastrous! The skill in beating is to trickle the birds over the guns in twos and threes, and to avoid the sudden massive flush which an uncontrolled dog can cause.

Most beaters, in addition to their dog, will also have a stick or a flag to tap ou the bushes or flag the birds forward. I you have not carried a stick before especially during training, your dog may be wary, but he will quickly get used to it A word of warning, however – never be tempted to use your stick on the dog in the heat of the moment. Apart from the damage you may do to him, it is quite easy to create avoiding action in your dog where he is reluctant to come anywhere near you when you are carrying a stick. I your dog needs a reprimand and you find yourself getting a little hot under the col-

Beaters in a narrow strip of kale. Notice the use of the flag, which dogs must become accustomed to.

lar, throw your stick to one side before moving forward to give the dog a shaking or a verbal berating. Punishment of your dog should be done at the time and scene of the crime, but it is certainly not acceptable in front of a team of Guns – a mild verbal reprimand would not be out of place but physical punishment would not gain any respect.

If your dog does something wrong, and one of the worst crimes is chasing after the birds or running in and collecting one that has been shot, it is better to play the situation quietly and calmly, calling the dog back to you where you can make him walk to heel or put him on a lead. Apologize to the keeper, and then work on the problem before the next shoot day. If your reaction to a dog's misbehaviour is to shout, whistle and chase, you will only bring further attention to yourself and your dog and make matters worse. Many times, when you are aware that your dog has done something wrong, no one else has noticed because they are all too involved with their own work. If there are occasions when you can correct your dog without causing offence or disruption, then certainly do so – otherwise the dog will quickly begin to realize that he can do what his heart desires when you are on a shoot because you do not reprimand him. However, if you have gained the respect of your dog, the verbal reproach and the 'look' should be sufficient.

A variety of dogs can be seen working in the beating line, from the pedigree gundog to the terrier and the crossbreed. In all cases, control of the dog is important, although on a shoot where there is very little game, the keeper may not worry too much provided that you find the game that is there. On the more formal shoots, where a large number of birds are present, control is essential, but you must decide on the type of dog you require. If there is a lot of heavy cover, a spaniel is the most obvious choice, although I have seen many retrievers making good in some of the heaviest cover. Because the retriever has a calmer, less exuberant hunting action, some people prefer them in the beating line, thinking that they can control them better. Others opt for the spaniel because of his optimistic attitude which will make him hunt out every piece of cover, always hoping for a find. Professional beaters' dogs have been trained without ever being allowed to retrieve – their whole life revolves around the hunt, the find and the flush. The temptation to chase, run forward on foot scent or look for a retrieve when they hear a shot is minimized. In the past, there were teams of dogs trained specifically for beating which were not allowed to retrieve, but today, few beaters can afford to have such a specialist dog, and their other pursuits dictate that he probably has to be a 'mutt of all trades'.

The number of beaters and the control of a beating line is very dependent upon the size of the shoot, the width of the drive and the terrain over which you are working. A gamekeeper will take charge of the line. Sometimes there will be a number of keepers in the line, but one will have the overall responsibility for the drive. When working in the beating line, know who that person is and make sure you listen to his commands. Sometimes you will be asked to hustle through particular areas and, on other occasions, to take things more easily, gently bringing forward the drive. If the beating line was run for the dogs it would progress at a speed which would allow your dog to make good all the ground – not leaving any tussock unsearched. However, this is not the case. If you do not think carefully,

Beating line under the control of one keeper working out a hedgerow.

and work accordingly, you can easily destroy the working pattern of your dog. With a spaniel, this can be very worrying, particularly if you also use him in competition. Where the line moves quickly over bare ground, it can be advantageous to pull your dog in to heel or put him on a lead. Start hunting him again once you are in cover and the line is walking forward at a speed where you can quarter the ground effectively. Even when the keepers are interested in the dogs and there is a willingness to let them work as they should, if there are a lot of dogs in the line they cover their ground at varying speeds. This can cause difficulties if the line is to stay straight.

In front of the line, game will be moving ahead, the scent will be hot, and many times birds will be in sight creating a high degree of temptation for your dog. Make sure that your dog is well under control and responding to the whistle before you take up a place in the beating line with him.

Not all dogs in the beating line are trained to a high standard and these will certainly be willing to teach your dog all the bad habits he would love to learn. Get to know what is expected of you and your dog from the keeper or other good dog people, and do not be tempted to go blithely on, following others who could easily be creating problems for you and your dog.

At the beginning of the drive, you may not encounter much game but as it progresses, you can expect the game to be concentrating in larger numbers ahead. You do not want to be flushing birds as you would on a rough shoot. By tapping sticks, making a noise and bustling your dog through the cover, you funnel the birds through a flushing point where they are encouraged to take off and fly over the waiting Guns.

Towards the end of the drive, the keeper in charge may command dogs to be brought to heel and the final few yards covered with just the tapping of sticks.

The aim is to have small flushes of birds flying in a steady stream over the guns rather than one large flush, which could be caused if a dog ran among the massed birds. During the hunt up with your dog, some birds will tuck in and be flushed by your dog. If they fly forward over the guns, or out to the side where a walking Gun could be placed, this is a bonus. If your dog does flush a bird, go through the discipline of making him sit to the flush, wait a few seconds before being given the command 'Gone Away' and carry on hunting. Should the bird fly out to the side of the drive and be shot, do not send your dog for the retrieve unless asked specifically to do so by the keeper in charge. If the bird is dead and you can pick it up easily by hand, this would be the best thing to do as it will discourage the dog from getting into the habit of thinking that he can retrieve birds from the beating line.

Although you will have spent a considerable amount of time training your dog and, possibly, introducing him to the real thing, the beating line is full of dangers. Good habits can be lost and bad ones introduced in the heat of the moment, particularly if you panic. It is imperative, therefore, that you introduce your dog carefully to beating, and by being aware of the nature of the job, carrying it out to the best of your ability while avoiding the pitfalls that are constantly present.

You should know your dog and be confident that you are the main interest in his life. If your dog is one who prefers the company of other dogs or is easily distracted from your control, the beating line will create difficulties for you. The beating line, in particular, demands that you are the centre of your dog's attention. Personally, I like a young dog to be so lacking in confidence initially that he is constantly looking to me for reassurance that all is well and that he is doing what I want. This is what many handlers would call a sticky dog. Very quickly, the dog will free up as he gains experience of beating, and will also gain good habits (if your handling develops them) through the additional training and control that comes with doing the work.

Initially, it may be helpful to put your dog on a lead and walk him in the line. In this way, he will experience other dogs and people, game being flushed and pushed ahead and the whole atmosphere of the day, while still being under close control. You can watch how the dog reacts and be relaxed, knowing that you are not going to get into any difficulties. There is no doubt that even walking the dog on the lead can be difficult when you have to negotiate obstacles or when the lead gets caught in brambles and bushes, but it will give you and your dog time to acclimatize to the scene and the noises. At the end of a drive, providing the time is available, you can let your dog off the lead and quietly work a corner out that has already been done. In this way, you will both gain confidence and you will be introducing your dog to hot scent, with little risk of live game being flushed as the cover has already been worked.

As you begin to trust your dog, and your own ability to handle him in the line, you can start to take him off the lead and let him hunt in front of you with the other dogs. Carefully select the places to do this. You do not want too much game, as this can get the dog too excited, but enough to get him hunting, and learning from the experience. Never be too proud to put your dog back on the lead if you feel the next drive may have too many birds or be difficult owing to the type of cover. Some cover can be very difficult to work while maintaining contact with your dog. High kale, thick rhododendrons, gorse and dense hedgerow can create problems demanding experienced dogs. Make sure that the keeper knows your limitations and put your dog on a lead or walk him to heel.

The main problem with these types of cover is that birds can run on ahead, and your dog, out of sight, can easily follow. If your dog is well under control and answering the whistle promptly, you can begin to hunt him in these covers, negotiating the vegetation in small stages and regularly regaining contact with him, either when he naturally comes looking for you or when you whistle him back. Some keepers may not mind your dog running way ahead or hunting freely in dense cover because there are few birds

and he wants to get them out, but if you succumb to this temptation you may develop bad habits. If asked to let your dogs run it out, agree to do so, but do i with the dog still under close control. I there is a large area to cover, work i systematically with your dog – and do no work him far away from you to save yourself the leg work. You may be asked to send your dog into a particular area and let him work it out. Do so, but go with your dog and work it out together. The only exception to this is if you are asked to send your dog on to a small island in the middle of a lake or river. But, again, only do this if your dog has the experience and maturity to do it.

Both in beating and picking up, I attempt to get into a position where the dog and I can do the work well, but can

Kale and roots can cause problems, but at the edges it is often shorter and young dogs can be worked and kept in view. A stick is also being used to help beat out the crop.

lso avoid potential problems. Whining nd giving tongue can be infectious, so if he neighbouring dog is doing this, move way from him. Some dogs hunt jealously, aking your dog's ground away from im, creating a nuisance or even showing ggression – again, try to get a place in the ine away from them. Some handlers are ery noisy and are not only constantly agging but even punishing their dogs; if ours is a sensitive dog, he can take this hreatening behaviour personally – keep our distance. If you have a good, observnt and dog-conscious keeper, he will elp you to do all this.

As I have mentioned previously, the eating line moves at a speed dictated by he keeper, which may not match your log's speed of hunting or give effective over of the ground you are working. If ou have been concentrating on thorough ;round cover and an effective hunting attern, moving forward too fast makes a onsense of your dog's efficiency. The eeper takes the wind into account only or the flying of the birds over the guns, ot for the scent and method of working our dog. You will have to do the best you an in these circumstances, while maintaining your position in the line. You must ealize that the keeper's primary interest is ot in your working your dog correctly but n doing the main job, which is to channel hose birds over the guns. To do this, he vill vary the speed and angles of the line – ou must work your dog and handle him o the best of your ability under the constraints that are imposed upon you.

Things happen very quickly in the beatng line and often, in the heat of the moment, all caution can disappear, so try o be a step ahead. Your experience will be a great asset in seeing what could and often does occur. Foresee potential problems and avoid them. Make your dog sit

and wait while you negotiate a fence or other obstacle. Insist that he sits, or at least stops, when he flushes a bird and that he waits for you to give the command 'Gone Away'. If you come across a large number of birds, make the dog sit and wait while you tap your stick and make them run ahead.

With time, your dog will gain experience, maturity and a knowledge of what is required. If you are consistent in your handling and gradually introduce the dog to new work and challenges, the work habits will be solidly ingrained, making him a very useful member of the beating team.

From the beating line you will often see the Guns and their shooting. No matter how you feel, you should never be critical of the Guns. It can be very frustrating at times to see a good drive wasted through poor shooting, but as long as you have done your job well, that is your only concern. On the other hand, I have seen the pleasure and pride of a Gun enhanced by beater's congratulating the shooting, even clapping, at the end of a drive. All behaviour is dependent upon the type of shoot and the relationship between the participants. If in doubt, play safe – be polite and concentrate only on doing your own job well.

As you come to the end of a drive, your dog may pick up birds that have been shot. If this happens, make sure that the keeper and any pickers-up know about it as it could save them a time-wasting search later on. Occasionally, a dog actually pegs a live bird that has not been shot. Although we do not want this to happen, it inevitably does when birds will not move or when they get themselves caught up, particularly in thick bramble or undergrowth. Some dogs can be commanded to drop such a bird but I prefer to call the

Little things matter – make the dog wait until you have got through a fence.

dog to me, take the bird and, after checking to ensure that it has not been previously shot, or damaged by the dog in extracting it from a bush, I release it. Unfortunately, there are dogs who try to catch live birds and become very adept at doing this, stalking and setting the birds before skilfully picking them. It is quite easy for you to read the actions that betray your dog's intentions so, as soon as you see this happening, stop him and tap out the bush or cover holding the bird. Better still, encourage your dog to flush the bird with a rapid continuous movement.

Pheasants are mainly running birds that can also fly and, therefore, tend to fly for only a short distance. In that distance they can use up a lot of energy. This means that they are not very keen on taking off and flying a second time, which makes them more peggable. Towards the end of the season, the birds become more wary and hens in particular tuck into cover rather than running or flying, which again makes them easy to peg. I remember one particular time when I was picking up with my black Labrador, Tinker. We had been asked to assist the walking Gun and were waiting next to him ready for the drive to start. I had sat Tinker and moved away from him to talk to the keeper and the Gun, and as the drive started I called him to me. As he returned to my side, he made a small detour to a patch of reeds very close to where he had been sitting; he gently put his head in them and carefully picked out a hen pheasant, proudly bringing it to me for all to see. The bird must have been there for close on ten minutes and Tinker had known that; I had no complaints about his nose or his handling of the bird but, none the less, it was a little embarrassing for me as the keeper was known to be very critical of dogs who peg birds.

Call your dog through afterwards.

Dogs who work regularly, occasionally peg a bird, and some become so adept at it that it can be a nuisance, but by reading your dog and having him under close control, you should be able to avoid many of the potential pegging opportunities. Many keepers are very understanding of this problem – as one told me, 'If they don't fly they are no good to me.'

Once the shoot is over, and you have all assembled back at the cars, the head keeper will bring you your fee for the day. Depending on the shoot, this may take the form of birds or money. The pay is not high but it helps to offset the cost of travelling to the shoot, and clothing to do the job. Some small shoots may not be able to give you anything but the pleasure of working your dog in good company and enjoying the sport – these shoots are often very rewarding in terms of a sense of belonging and team friendship. Any-one who beats just for money will be very disappointed.

At the end of a hard beating day, care for your dog first. Often he is wet as well as tired, and a towelling followed by something warm to lie on in your car will help relax the muscles and minimize the chance of rheumatism. A drying bag, dry hay or straw, or wood wool in a dog box are all good ways of helping your dog recover from the strain of the day. Although you may have checked him over during the day, check him over again when you get home and are in good light. Remove any tangles and foreign bodies caught up in the fur or attached to the body; and clean and deal with any grazes or minor cuts (serious cuts should be dealt with by your vet). A warm meal and a warm bed then provides the perfect end to a dog's day.

6 Picking Up

Picking up is becoming as much of a sport as the shooting of game itself. Working together with your dog in challenging situations to retrieve what could otherwise be difficult or irretrievable shot game can give you a tremendous amount of pleasure and satisfaction. Picking up is an art built upon the skills of dog and man, and developed through experience and a knowledge of countryside and wildlife. For many gundog owners, it is towards this that they are working when training their dog, building a partnership that will work for Gun and keeper to ensure that

Working an older, experienced dog with a young dog on the lead.

shot game is brought to bag and the suffering of wounded game is minimized.

Obtaining picking-up work is not easy and, although everyone has to learn, including their dog, keepers require experienced pickers-up and dogs who earn their reward whether it be in cash, birds or both. Therefore, if you are inexperienced and your dog is the same, it may be very difficult to get started, unless you have good contacts within the business. If you have a small shoot of your own, or have a gun on one, you may be able to get the required experience and also the necessary contacts; in fact, it is a great advantage to have had shooting experience before picking up – it will give you insight into the Gun's view of shooting and picking up and also enable you to know their thoughts on the work that is required. It will also give you the experience required to spot the birds that are pricked and are likely to become runners, requiring extra attention and effort from you and your dog to put them in the bag.

If you have contacts with keepers or shooting syndicates, one way to get the initial experience is to offer your assistance free of charge. It is most helpful if you have a friend with experienced dogs who is already picking up on the shoot and under whose guidance you can become a trainee. It must be remembered that a shoot is the keeper's livelihood and, as such, all the work related to a shoot day must be done well to ensure a successful and enjoyable day for the Guns. Although you will be training your dog further

If you have two dogs, make sure that
they are both obedient and under
control.

Make sure that your dog is familiar with farm animals.

while picking up, you are employed on the shoot to do a job of work and therefore must do it to the best of your ability. If you do not take any reward until you can perform a worthwhile task, and if there is always an experienced picker-up with you to make sure the job is effectively carried out, the keeper will generally accept you – it may be to his future benefit. However you start picking up, it is important to realize that you are part of a team and must work as such.

When your dog has become experienced and you are part of the picking-up team, continue to do the job that the keeper expects of you. Some handlers who enjoy running their dogs in competition have earned themselves bad reputations by using the job just to develop their dog for competition work. Retrieves that may prove awkward or, they feel, could spoil their dog are avoided, and they may spend a considerable amount of time handling their dog on to an easy dead bird as part of a training exercise, while other birds go unpicked. If you are concerned about causing any problems by using your dog for a particular piece of work, have an older, more experienced dog available to do the job – one who will not spoil. In general, I have found that providing you use some common sense, there are very few situations that need to be avoided. If your dog is experienced and under control, which a competition dog should be, he should be able to deal with any request with your assistance.

Once you have an experienced dog who can handle the work, and your skills become known, you will begin to receive invitations to pick up on other shoots. It is a fact that although picking-up work is difficult to obtain, good pickers-up are in short supply.

Your first day picking up on a shoot will often cause you some concern, mainly

Friendliness with a Gun is not always encouraged on some commercial shoots. However, find out how the Gun would like you to pick his birds.

Patiently waiting during a drive. Game bag for carrying bits and pieces.

because you want to do well and be asked back again. The day is provided for the Guns, and their pleasure and the keeper's satisfaction is what you are working for. Therefore, consideration, politeness and an efficient background role will pay dividends. No matter what happens, hold your own counsel: if there is something which you feel is wrong or particularly unsafe, have a quiet word with the keeper. Find out what the form is on the shoot and what is expected of you.

Your first shoot, even if it is a small one, can be confusing, and it is quite easy to lose yourself both mentally and physically. A map showing the drives on the shoot is always helpful, together with a list of them and the order in which they will be shot. Find out if there are any limitations to the picking that you will be doing – for example, there may be double drives at one stand. This is where, after driving the birds from one area over the Guns, the Guns then about face and the birds are driven from a beat that was behind them. Picking up in the area of the second beat would therefore be put off until this drive had been completed. Where this occurs, always ask the beaters as they complete the drive if they have picked any birds on the way through – it could save you a long fruitless search.

There are certain pieces of equipment that will prove invaluable and also ease the job of picking up. A pencil and paper wrapped in a polythene bag (to keep them dry) are useful to make the occasional note and also, on drives where large numbers of birds are shot, to draw a sketch of the area and mark on it the position of the birds as they fall. A knife and some baler twine can be invaluable for a variety of jobs, particularly for tying together braces of birds to make them easier to carry and hang in the game cart. There are a variety

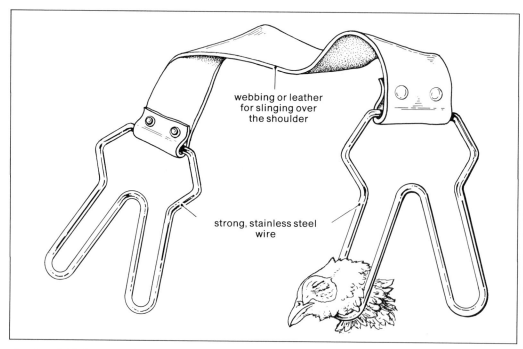

Figs 9 and 10 Game carriers.

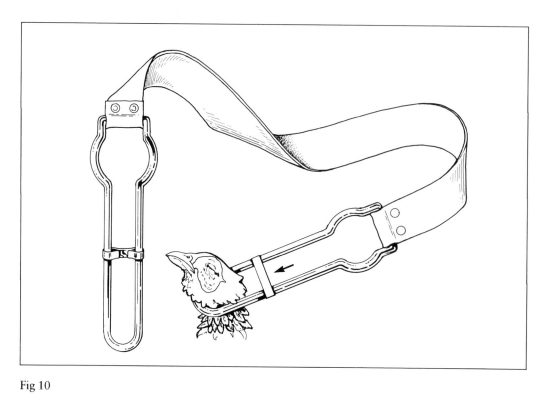

Fig 10

A good way of holding a wounded bird to minimize its struggling.

of game carriers on the market, used to hold the dead game. They can be slung over your shoulder or carried like bags, enabling you to carry far more game than you could by hand. A vital piece of equipment is a device for helping you to dispatch game. I favour a 'priest', a small, weighted truncheon which is used to hit the animal behind the head, quickly killing it.

No sportsman likes to wound game, but it does happen and as a picker-up you will have to deal with wounded game quickly and humanely. For pheasant, partridge and other small birds, the priest is ideal – a sharp and powerful blow to the back of the head will fracture the skull or sever the spinal cord. Death from this method should be instantaneous. In delivering the blow, it is necessary to hold the bird still. If you hold either the body in the crook of your arm or the wings, which you hold together above the body, this should stop the bird struggling and bring the head forward into a suitable position for the blow. One technique that some people employ is to grasp the head and twirl the bird around by the neck giving it a sharp jerk upwards. I find this method to be not only distasteful, but also very ineffective and I would certainly not recommend it. There are other methods, such as fracturing the skull with the thumb-nail, but I have never been successful at administering them. If you do not have a priest with you, a good stout walking stick will do the job. Another alternative is to swing the bird by the body to give the head a good blow against a fence post or tree. This, I also find distasteful, and I would only use it if I did not have a priest or stick with me.

Ducks and geese can be particularly difficult to dispatch and it is worth taking lessons from more experienced members of the shoot on the best ways of dealing

Fig 11   Bird held firmly by the wings; head naturally goes out straight. A sharp knock is delivered to the head with the priest.

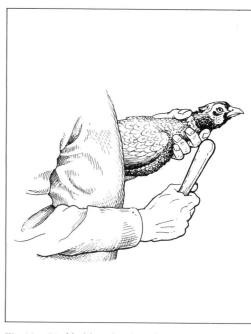

Fig 12   Bird held under the left arm while the left hand holds head forward. Sharp knock to the head with the priest.

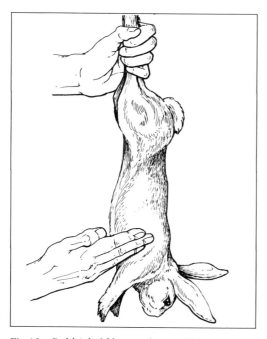

Fig 13   Rabbit held by rear legs and hit on the back of the head with the priest or chopped with the side of the hand.

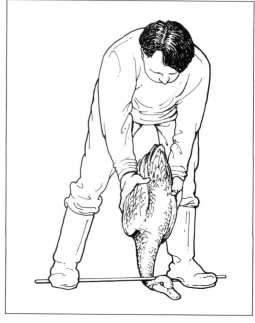

Fig 14   Stick laid across neck of duck. The body is jerked sharply upwards to dislocate the neck.

with them. A sharp blow from a priest can do the job but with their long necks it is more difficult to administer. They also seem to have far stronger skulls than pheasants. Using your hands to dislocate the neck is possible with practice. However, another way of achieving this is to lay the head carefully on the ground and place a stick across it; put a foot either side of the head on top of the stick and holding the body firmly give a sharp upward pull to dislocate the neck.

Rabbits and hares can also be killed using the priest. Hold the animal by the back legs so that its body hangs down and give a sharp blow with the priest or the side of your hand in a chopping motion.

The Semark dispatching tool which can be obtained from some gunshops and the British Association for Shooting and Conservation provides a very humane and quick means of dispatching game and would repay your investment if you are inexperienced at dealing with wounded game. The Game Conservancy at Fordingbridge, Hampshire, have issued a leaflet explaining the ways in which game can be dispatched and, if you have any doubts, it would be worth sending for it. If you are to pick up, it is essential that you not only become adept at handling dead game but also at dealing with wounded game. Initially, you may feel a little squeamish, but it is only humane and respectful to the game to deal with them and dispatch them quickly, competently and humanely.

On some shoots the keeper will give the pickers-up instructions, on others there will be a chief picker-up. On some, the pickers-up have done the job so many times that they do it without thinking. Whatever the situation, the keeper will generally put you right, but if he is busy or unavailable, a word with a regular picker-up will provide you with the relevant information. You may be provided with transport, if it is required, but this is not always the case and on occasions you may be expected to use your own vehicle. Lunch may not seem a priority until your stomach begins to tell you otherwise. Before the day of the shoot, find out what the routine is for lunch and prepare accordingly. There is nothing worse than being tired after a long morning's work and then discovering that you have no lunch.

Working as a picker-up, you need to be in a position that will allow you to see where shot birds are falling, but which is also safe. The exact position depends on the type of country being shot over. On a pheasant shoot, it is worth while having some of the picking-up team standing well back – maybe even a few hundred yards behind the Guns – from where the whole proceedings can be watched. From such a vantage point, pricked birds (which can glide for a considerable distance) can be marked and, quite often, picked up and dealt with swiftly without disturbing the shooting that is in progress.

Partridge and grouse tend to fly low to the ground and Guns will regularly swing round to take a shot at a departing bird. A position that is either a considerable distance behind a Gun or in the line of guns is the safest and will allow the Guns to shoot without worrying about peppering a picker-up. If there are a number of pickers-up, you can split up the team to the best advantage, some standing close to the line where they can see what is happening and others way back, even out of sight of the Guns, to watch for the pricked birds. Woodland shoots, where Guns stand in cuttings and the birds fly from woodland in front of them to wood-

On a partridge drive, the picker-up and dogs are better placed between the Guns.

land behind, need this organization. Some pickers-up may stand just inside the wood behind the Guns while others stand outside the wood, watching for the birds which have been wounded. If there is a release pen in the woods, it is likely that the birds will make for this, and a picker-up standing within the pen can quickly spot and deal with wounded birds as they land.

Some wounded birds can easily be identified – they have dropped a leg, their flight is erratic, the wing beat sounds different or their landing is clumsy. Other birds may tower (fly upwards before falling to the ground) and are usually dead on landing. However, there are shot birds that show no sign of being wounded, although a brief search of the area where they have landed will result in your dog picking them because they are weak. An experienced dog can often sense a wounded bird even though you may

think that it is unharmed. Watch your dog and use his animal instinct to find the ones that have been wounded. After all, that is what you are there for. I have seen a number of 'old timers' watch a bird in flight and the handler, recognizing the look in the eye of the dog, sends him, trusting the dog's instinct. More often than not, the dog returns with a bird that has been hit. When a bird is dead in the air, its head flies back and there is a puff of feathers from the front of the body. If the rear end flips, then the shot has hit too far back to kill instantly. In some cases, the bird will fly on, but the wing beat becomes almost silent. Often these birds will be found dead, although one wise old picker-up once told me, 'A bird isn't dead until it's in the oven.' Having seen a number of 'dead' birds, particularly duck, make miraculous recoveries in game bags and game carts, I know what he meant.

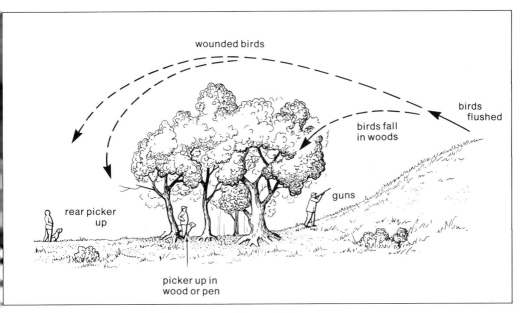

wounded birds

birds
flushed

birds fall
in woods

guns

rear picker
up

picker up in
wood or pen

Fig 15   Large formal shoot. Pickers-up in wood are well back.

Become adept at remembering where birds fall and marking the place by means of landmarks such as unusually shaped trees, telegraph poles, marks on the horizon, fence posts and other such objects.

Wherever you stand, it is a good idea to let the Gun know that you are there. Wearing countryside clothing, you can easily merge into the background and an eager Gun could shoot in your direction, thinking it is safe. If you are close to a Gun, ask him if he is happy with your position and be prepared to move to a spot where you will not be a hindrance to him. Once the Gun knows where you are, it is not a good idea to move about. If you have to move, make sure that you do not place yourself in a vulnerable position.

Find out when and where you can pick up if you do not know – different shoots have different ideas. If in doubt, always wait until the end of the drive before sending your dog for any bird (unless it is a runner and the situation demands that it is picked immediately). Sending your dog among the Guns to pick should not be done, particularly if the birds are dead. Even if there is a runner, watch where it runs and enters cover and wait until the end of the drive before attempting the retrieve. Many runners will tuck in when they reach cover and can, therefore, be picked later. If you send your dog for a runner among the Guns and he makes a bad job, possibly even giving chase into the present drive where he prematurely flushes birds waiting to be pushed over the Guns, you will not be very popular.

Find out how you will know when the drive is over. In the majority of cases, the head keeper will give a signal: a horn blast, a long blast from a particularly audible whistle or the cry 'All Out!'. On some shoots, he may not signal the end of the drive at all, in which case it is advis-

85

Sending a dog, like the one in the foreground here, for dead birds amongst the Guns should not be done.

able that you keep the Guns in view in order to see what the state of play is. When the shooting stops, it may only be a lull in the proceedings and not the time to start working your dog. The other reason for keeping an eye on the Guns in such a situation is that it has been known for a picker-up to be left behind. If you are that person and you do not know the ground, and the keeper does not know where you have been left, it can be a little embarrassing, even frightening – funny afterwards, perhaps, but not at the time!

Many Guns like to bring a dog with them on to the shoot. Unfortunately, these are often the most unruly and badly controlled dogs there, but it is not your place to voice such an observation and criticize. If a Gun has a dog, make it a point to ask if he wishes to pick up with his dog after the drive and if there are any birds that he would not wish to send his dog for. Some Guns have young dogs and will not wish

to pick any birds, others will pick the ones in close proximity to the peg and ask you to deal with the more distant birds or the runners. Other Guns will wish to pick the majority of the birds they shoot and ask you to retrieve only the ones that are runners and could possibly become irretrievable if not promptly dealt with.

A Gun with a dog should not be viewed as a nuisance, but someone to work with who has priority in the picking. As the drive is in progress, you can often mark the fall of the birds much better than the Gun and, by watching his dog work after the drive, know whether any have been left. If you assist the Gun and help him to enjoy working his dog, you will often find that he begins to ask you to take certain retrieves, and a very pleasurable piece of teamwork develops. As I have mentioned, though, some dogs are not good and need to be watched. A dog who picks a bird and then drops it in another place to pick a second bird, and who continues to play this game, can be a nuisance. Watch what is happening and wait until the Gun and his dog move away before working the area to find the birds.

Once a Gun with a dog appears to have finished picking and moves away, you can sweep through with your dog and see if any have been left. A polite word with the Gun does not go amiss – ask him if he thinks the area is clear and whether you could run your dog through just to check that nothing has come down unseen.

Guns without dogs should be easier to work with, but again make sure that the Gun is not one who likes to pick a few of his birds by hand. If you are close to the Gun, you can ask him whether he wants you to pick his birds for him or, if you are a distance from the Gun, you can watch what he does at the end of the drive to determine how you should approach the picking. Some Guns walk away from their pegs and take no interest in the picking of the birds; others enjoy watching their birds being picked, considering it to be part of the enjoyment of the day. Count the birds you have seen down and, as you pick them, make a mental note of what they were (particularly sex and colour) and where you picked them. Compare notes with an interested Gun and work together to ensure that, as far as possible, nothing is left.

Often, the Gun will have to leave you to the picking and move to another drive. If you find birds after he has left, make a note of the retrieves and give him this information at a convenient opportunity. A Gun will particularly like to know whether you have found a runner, and will definitely want to know if you have found the woodcock he shot. If you could not find a specific bird do not be afraid to tell him, and also tell the keeper about it

so that at a free moment, either later in the day or the next morning, he can also have a search for the bird. If a bird has eluded you and you have to move on to the next drive, it shows enthusiasm if you return to have another search either in the lunch break or, if the keeper gives you permission, at the end of the day. It is quite surprising how a bird you could not find earlier often comes to hand if you return later and work systematically without any time pressures. If you think that there are birds down, when the Guns are moving off to the next drive, and you have enough pickers-up in the team, it is a good idea to leave one or two of them behind to finish the job before meeting up with you later.

Birds that are difficult to find often attract other dog handlers who are quick to throw their dogs into the search. I personally find this eagerness to 'beat you to the bird' very annoying and, unless a number of dogs can work individual beats without interfering with each other, I ask other pickers-up to keep out of the way and give my dogs a chance first. Too many dogs running about over the same ground not only fouls the area (confuses the scent so that it is impossible to follow) but means they do not concentrate on their work. If your dog is not successful, do not be too proud to ask someone else to try with his dog; but if it appears as though a free for all is happening, call your dog out of the pack and find another area to work.

One position that many pickers-up prefer is with a walking Gun. This is where a Gun walks along the flanks of the beating line to take any birds that emerge from the sides and would probably fly back behind the beating line. With dog at heel, you walk at the same pace as the Gun, either with him or at a certain dis-

Picker-up with walking Gun carrying extra cartridges and gun case.

tance behind, depending on the ground and how easy it is to watch the birds down. Not knowing the flight path of the birds, it is often more advantageous to walk close to the Gun, but a respectful distance behind. If you are asked to walk along with the Gun, perhaps even to show him the way, do make sure that you do not hinder his shooting in any way and be ready either to crouch down or move out of the way should the need arise. If you are asked to attend the walking Gun, it is both courteous and helpful to his shooting if you offer to carry his gun case and cartridge bag. If you have to leave to find a runner or distant bird, check on your return that nothing else has been shot during your absence. A real partnership can be created between a picker-up and a walking Gun, as both are working for each other alone. A good shot followed by an equal retrieve, or a difficult one on a strong runner, can form a rewarding

bond between the two people and dog involved.

Where a number of pickers-up are used, each handler will have an allocated area. Stick to your own area and make sure that birds in that area are picked first before moving on and asking other handlers, who may have more birds to deal with, whether they need any help. Do not go picking other birds that fall in the area of fellow pickers-up. If they have marked these birds down they will not thank you if you pick them without their knowledge and they then hunt for non-existent retrieves. More important, each picker-up will consider birds falling in his area to be his property and take great exception to being denied a retrieve for his dog. Do not go retrieving other handlers' birds or runners unless they ask you to do so. If there are not many birds down and one in your area is an easy retrieve for you but a testing one for your neighbour's dog, provided that it does not delay you or interfere with the shoot, why not offer him the retrieve? He will soon learn to reciprocate and you will both get enjoyable dog work.

During the drive, you may notice birds that have been shot and have fallen in areas other than the one for which you are directly responsible. It often happens that, because of your angle of view, you can see birds shot when others cannot. Watch these birds and notice how they come down. Did they tower (fly on as though unshot and then suddenly fly upwards gaining height, usually without moving forward) before falling to the ground? Generally, this is caused by a lung shot and the bird will be found dead where it fell. Notice the hit bird that drops a leg. These birds should not be able to move far from the fall area. By being observant and thinking about the

situation, you will gain invaluable experience that will enable you to help your dog find all types of shot bird. After you have worked your own area, ask other handlers if they noticed and picked any of these potentially elusive birds that you watched coming down.

Prior to picking up, your dog should have undergone training to bring him up to a standard where he can be handled under control among live game. However, the real thing does create a different environment and not only can your dog behave in a way that is out of character but so also can you. At all times endeavour to make as little noise as possible, whether you are moving into position prior to a drive or handling your dog after the drive has finished. Noisy handling can not only disturb game but will also bring others' attention to the difficulties you are

Hunting up hedgerows for unseen shot birds after a drive.

encountering. Quiet handling might not get you noticed, but if you bring in the game and ensure that the Guns know you have picked the dead and runners which they have shot, you will be valued far more highly and stay on the shoot longer.

Your dog will develop his nose and become experienced more quickly by working on birds he cannot see. Birds lying dead in a field in full view can be picked by yourself or other members of the shoot. Work your dog on birds that demand the natural abilities and senses he possesses. Develop in your dog a free-hunting ability to sweep areas which may contain birds that have not been precisely marked. Sweeping an area with a hunting dog is an essential part of picking up. Once you have picked those birds that were marked down, you will be surprised how many more will be found by a meth-odical hunt in the fall area. On commercial shoots, Guns usually pay for their day according to the number of birds shot and this provides the income for the shoot. Therefore, the keeper and shoot owner will want every bird shot accounted for. By sweeping the area, even though it may be thought all birds have been picked you will be showing your commitment to the success of the shoot and there is no doubt that this will be noticed. While you are sweeping, make sure that you investigate every piece of cover, no matter how small. It is quite surprising how birds can disappear into the smallest tussock. They may disappear from sight but not from the nose of your dog.

As you get to know the shoot, you will become aware of problem areas and also dangers. Barbed-wire fences; steep drops, even cliffs; estate rubbish tips full of

After a drive, make sure you have not left anything behind, by sweeping through woodland for shot birds.

Never be too proud to put an inexperienced dog on a lead during
tempting moments.

broken glass; trap lines where snares, though lifted, can still catch a dog's foot; and roads are all potential danger zones for your dog and need to be handled with care and common sense. Prior to every drive, if you do not already know, ask if there are any no-go areas for using your dog – these will include future drives, pens of birds and, occasionally, a neighbour's land where relationships may not be cordial.

In the course of picking up, you may encounter new and difficult retrieves. Hares, woodcock and snipe, for example, can create difficulties for the inexperienced dog and handler. It is advisable to ask for another shot to be put into a wounded hare, if safe to do so. Wounded hares can squeal quite frighteningly and alarm an inexperienced dog, putting him

off retrieving them in future. Woodcock and snipe are not always easy to locate and some dogs find them distasteful at first. Where these have been shot and retrieved by other dogs, ask if you can use them to provide a quick training retrieve for your dog in order to accustom him to the experience. If your dog is unsure of the bird, a quick rub over with your hands and a little teasing of the dog with the bird, before throwing it, generally gets the desired result. Should you be asked to retrieve game you have not picked before, and you think there could be problems, do not be too proud to mention this and ask for a more experienced dog to help you.

As your dog gains experience and you gain confidence both in the dog and in yourself, you will be able to handle a

Young inexperienced dogs can have difficulty carrying large cock pheasants and will bring them with any convenient mouth hold. They will soon learn how to carry correctly.

multitude of situations. You will also be able to read all the messages that your dog is sending you during his work. If you ever err, do so on the side of trusting your dog and his instincts – you will be constantly amazed and fascinated at what he can do, and particularly at how often he proves you wrong. Experienced dogs often notice a pricked bird, which you do not; do not pull them off the line of the runner that you thought was a dead bird; and if you think your dog has suddenly gone rabbiting, put your hand down the hole to make sure the 'rabbit' is not the bird you are after, gone to ground.

Make it a habit to check every bird your dog retrieves to you for damage that could have been caused by him. A dog is said to be hard-mouthed when, in retrieving a bird, he bites and damages it. If your dog damages every bird he retrieves, the value of the birds is dramatically reduced both commercially and as food. Whether you continue to use your dog as a retriever of birds when he consistently damages them is your decision. Personally, I would not. To check a bird for damage that is not obviously visible, lay it on its back in the palm of your right hand with the head away from your body. With your other hand, press down gently on the breast bone and, with the right hand, feel the ribs. You will notice if any are collapsed or broken.

Although hard-mouth is a serious fault, and a dog who is known to have it should not be used for breeding purposes, many dogs will damage birds occasionally or bring back damaged birds. You should not condemn your dog out of hand for

To test for hard-mouth, lay the bird breast upwards in the palm of your hand, thumb one side, fingers the other.

Gently feel along the ribs. A little pressure on the breast bone will help locate any damage.

this without looking at how it happened. At the beginning of the season, young birds are delicate and easily damaged; dogs may be inexperienced or very keen, or both, which can result in ribs being broken or put in. Birds can also be easily damaged if they fall onto frosty ground, ground containing a lot of flint or stones, or if they fall into woodland when a collision with a tree trunk or branch can do a lot of harm. Also, watch how the bird was shot – if it was shot at close range or received the shot all in one side, the shot itself can easily damage the ribs. The other situation to watch for is where the dog has had problems extracting the bird from cover or out of a hole. A strong runner may take some catching and holding, causing tearing and damage at the rear end of the bird.

Do not be concerned if your dog has the odd problem bird but, if it is the norm, you will have to consider what should be done about it. Bad breeding, poor training or a sudden occurrence in the shooting field can cause a dog to squeeze birds. A strong cock pheasant will often spur a dog in its attempt to escape. Naturally, the dog does not like this and bites the bird, which dies and no longer uses its spurs. In this, the dog has learnt an unwanted lesson. I was once judging a spaniel trial in Dorset and, upon testing a cock pheasant that had just been retrieved, found it was damaged on one side. The dog had only been working for a short time and the gun was quite close to where the bird had fallen, so I gave the dog the benefit of the doubt, made a note in my book and let him continue. Within a short distance another cock was shot, this time not too close, and it fell into a grass field. The dog successfully retrieved the bird but, again, it was damaged – this time on both sides. I took the bird to my co-judge for his opinion, which was the same as mine – the dog was hard-mouthed. I then showed the competitor the bird and told him my decision. At this, he told me that the dog had only just started damaging birds, but added that these were only ever cocks. Perhaps he was hoping to have hens for the retrieves on this day!

There are various problems that your dog can come up against during a day's picking up. The most obvious is that he will be faced with large numbers of birds – in some instances, perhaps, too many. Excitement and confusion in the dog can be transferred to you, so keep calm, control yourself and your dog, and give yourself time to deal with the situation. If you are working your dog on a retrieve and, while disobeying you, he finds a bird in a different direction from the one you were trying to send him to, he may now think

that he knows better than you or is confused because he found a retrieve while working against your commands. If you work the dog too long on a retrieve that cannot be found, the dog can lose confidence and enthusiasm. It is a good idea always to carry a spare bird with you, which you can drop when the dog is not looking and then let him search for it and succeed in finding it. A problem you will face as a handler is how to determine exactly where a bird fell if it dropped out of sight behind a wood or over a hedge. How far did the bird glide before it hit the ground – was it a few yards or a hundred? It can be difficult to estimate.

As part of the picking-up team, you are a small part of the whole organization which comprises the shoot. Everyone is there for a purpose and, to be successful, you must always work together. It is

As a picker-up, you are part of a team and should work as one.

Make sure that all birds are taken to the game cart and not left around
the pegs or on the field.

In the rush of activity, never forget to praise your dog for doing a good
job.

worth while to know more about what others do towards the shoot day, what they want out of it and what is expected of them. Put yourself in their wellies and gain an understanding of all aspects of a shoot. The knowledge will help you to make your day a more rewarding experience and can save you hours of frustration and irritability.

At the end of the day, make sure that you have put all the birds you have picked onto the game cart. Offer to help carry the birds from the game cart to the game larder, and ask if there is anything else that the keeper would like you to do before you set off home. Do not forget the 'thank you' – if you have had a good day and enjoyed it, show your appreciation.

Once home, the most important job is to ensure that your dog is comfortable. Check him over for any cuts or nasty scratches, clean them and apply antiseptic lotion or powder; remove burrs, brambles and other bits from his coat; give him a good meal; and then, after a short exercise to answer the call of nature, make sure he has a warm bed to curl up into.

7 The Gun's Dog – Formal Shoots

The working standard of most gundogs brought to a shoot as a companion to a Gun is generally poor, even though the work they do is limited and they do not require a wide variety of skills. On the smaller shoots, a Gun's dog may have to pick up all of his handler's birds and be trained to deal with a multitude of situations, but on the larger formal shoots this is not usually the case.

On a large shoot, the Gun's dog is required to be steady to shot and be able to withstand the temptations that go with large numbers of shot birds falling around him. He is usually only required to retrieve a few birds that have fallen around the peg area and these he will have seen falling, although, if there was a large number, he will not have remembered every one. Between drives, the dog will be required to walk quietly at heel and not make a nuisance of himself with game or other guests. It should not be too much to ask of a gundog, but how many times have you seen a Gun's dog run in at every bird shot – and not just his owner's birds? If he is fastened to the peg to stop him running in, he then whines, yelps or barks, and I have even seen the corkscrew pegs that have been specifically made to hold dogs pulled out of the ground in the excitement of the moment with a bung of earth still attached. When sent for a bird, the dog is out of control the moment the lead is taken off. The Gun handles the

situation either by completely ignoring it and hoping that the dog will not find a runner that takes him into the next drive or by shouting and becoming heated in an attempt to get the dog to do something right.

I can remember, at more than one shoot, seeing dogs fastened to their owners while they were shooting. In one instance, the dog was attached to the owner's leg. Picturing the owner being dragged across a field by a dog in pursuit of a bird is amusing, but it is a very dangerous thing to do with a loaded gun in the hand.

Perhaps it is the bad dogs whom we remember, but there is no need to have a bad dog if you approach the training correctly and if, when taking him into the field in the early days, you make it a priority to concentrate on the dog and give him your full attention – this is even more important than the shooting. A bad dog always gives you something to talk about and, for some reason, many Guns seem almost to take pride in being able to tell a story about their dog, which makes him the worst dog in the pack. Perhaps by talking and joking about it, such people believe that other Guns will accept the misdemeanours as something to laugh about and, because they admit to the faults and make fun of them, they will not be thought of as fools. After the occurrence, one can always laugh, but

The Gun's dog, steady and controlled under fire and in company.

The Gun's dogs waiting patiently until called to heel.

when it is actually happening, it might not be so funny.

The formal Gun's dog needs to be a companion; he must be sociable and be able to mix in company, but he must not be a nuisance (in any way). He must be steady in 'hot corners' and under control, and he should be able to retrieve shot birds that have fallen within a short distance of the peg. As a Gun with a dog, it should give you as much pleasure and pride to handle a good dog as it does to shoot a good bird. The dog should make the Gun's day, and not spoil it for others.

Before taking your dog to a formal shoot, get to know what is considered to be good form. Leave your dog in the car until required; if he needs to have a stretch and answer the call of nature, make sure he does it safely, away from any of the day's drives and the owner's lawn or paths. Ask where the next drive will be so that you know where it is safe to send your dog for a retrieve, and know where the pickers-up are situated. The picker-up should wait for you to retrieve those birds that you want. If he does not, do not be afraid to ask him to wait until you have finished. The picker-up should take the ones that have fallen well behind the line and the runners that would otherwise escape if not picked promptly. Dead birds around the peg should not be picked until the end of the drive. If your dog is young and you only want a few retrieves and not live birds, tell the picker-up and ask him to deal with the difficult ones. A good picker-up will respect and be pleased to work with a Gun who knows what is expected and handles his dog well.

In training your dog, concentrate especially on the obedience and discipline exercises: walking to heel; sits and stays; seen retrieves and good direct returns to hand; and coming immediately when called. Very rarely do Guns go in for hand signals and so the dog should be able to work on his own initiative, but again I emphasize, under control and obedient when required.

Never send a novice dog for a retrieve during a drive, even if a runner comes down – you should have an experienced dog or a picker-up with such a dog to handle these birds. If shooting over your dog, a firm 'No' or 'Stay' to reaffirm your control prior to taking a shot, does not go amiss, and lets the dog know that you are still concentrating on him. Many dogs I have introduced to the field never get a retrieve on a bird they have seen fall until they have sat through a number of drives and, as I do not have them on every drive during a shoot day, it may

Working two dogs can be fun and rewarding provided they have been well schooled.

Accustom your dog to feather in preparatory training by attaching wings to dummies.

If your dog has problems carrying a warm retrieve, place an elastic band around a freshly shot bird to make a tight package which is easier to hold.

not be until the third or fourth outing that they are allowed this experience. After a drive is over, I leave the dog sitting and pick up the dead birds by hand, letting the dog watch me do this and also making sure he watches other dogs working. Once all the birds have been picked, I will then go through a simple, familiar training exercise using a warm bird. Generally, there are few problems in getting your dog to pick a warm bird if he has already handled cold ones, but if you do experience difficulty, rub your hands over the bird and show it to him prior to throwing it and then encourage him to return the moment his head goes down to pick it. Duck can cause a few problems, but by making this first retrieve fun, and keeping calm, you can quickly overcome them. The first 'real' retrieve on a freshly shot bird

should be a simple one where your dog can succeed quickly without your getting hot under the collar. Runners will come later with experience and steadiness. If something does go wrong, try to handle it as calmly as possible. Was it just an unfortunate occurrence or have you missed out on some of your dog's early training?

At all times during the first days, keep your eye on your dog and read his behaviour. Watch for nervousness, which may occur if a barrage of shots are suddenly fired, and be on hand to reassure. Be aware of heightened enthusiasm which can result in him becoming over excited. Calm him down and never be too proud to put him back in the car for the next drive or even for the rest of the day. Read your dog at all times and make sure that he knows you are aware of his thoughts and

A Gun with two dogs, one a youngster and one an old hand. Notice that the younger dog is sitting close where there is better control and contact.

actions. By keeping one step ahead and channelling all the dog's natural instincts into doing the right thing, you can build the basics into a solid, working foundation.

At the end of the day, I should be surprised if you did not see the need for a little additional training. However, when everything has gone well and Guns voice their praises of this paragon of virtue, you may well be proud; but be doubly observant and prompt next time because, by then, your dog will know a little bit more and be just a little more keen!

Most well-bred gundogs are easily introduced to the gun through gradual progression from a loud handclap to the starting pistol, and then on to the twelve-bore. However, like every other aspect of training, you can create problems, which you then have to work at to overcome. Often the problem is caused by your doing something that frightens the dog, and which the dog will then associate with the shot. I have often heard of people taking their dogs to a game shoot or a clay shoot to get them accustomed to the sound of gunfire. If this is your approach, maybe you have been lucky and the dog has taken it in his stride; but many dogs who may accept one shot the first time they hear it, experience stress and fear when it is followed by a number of other shots, such as occur on a formal shoot.

Quite a few young dogs are nervous when they first hear a shot. This should not be taken as chronic gun-shyness, as they will doubtless overcome it. You must ensure that your own anxiety at your dog's apparent nervousness of shot does not actually create gun-shyness. A really gun-shy dog will never overcome that fear of the gun.

Even though your dog may appear confident and unconcerned at the sound of gunfire, you must still be aware of the situations which could create problems. A grouse-butt can concentrate the noise, and if a considerable number of shots are fired in rapid succession, this could quite easily frighten your dog. Woodland and valleys create echoes and unusual sounds, which can also worry a dog with sensitive hearing. I have a ten-year-old spaniel, a hardened campaigner of many a shooting day who still regularly picks up and works to the gun for me, but if he hears a gun fired around my house, he disappears into the dining room and hides under the table. I am uncertain why he does this. The only reason I can put forward is that we live in a wooded area in a slight valley, which creates an echo. It is sometimes difficult to determine where noises are coming from, and gunfire does sound quite different in our grounds compared to the open shooting field. I know for certain that if he hears gunfire when he is out with me on a shoot, the reaction is completely different – his face becomes full of anticipation and interest, not concern and fear.

For some dogs, the fear is not of the sound, but of the gun itself. The sound of gunfire in itself does not worry them, but when this is coupled with a gun being raised close to them, they disappear to the car or the kennel. It has been suggested by others that dogs associate a raised gun with a stick raised to hit them, but I think this is the exception rather than the rule. There must be something in the dog's mental make-up which brings about this fear. Perhaps it is also hereditary – I am sure that puppies inherit many of their parents' fears, phobias, likes and loves.

If your dog has this particular problem, introduce the swinging gun in stages.

Firstly, swing your arms above the dog's head prior to throwing dummies or while getting him to sit and stay. Once you are confident that this causes no distress, take a stick out with you and swing this about, gradually using it as a pretend gun. You can also use a starting pistol to fire the occasional shot in conjunction with the arm and stick movements. Finally, take a gun out and go through the actions of shooting. If at any time you see any concern, go back a step to where the dog was happy, and gradually build up again. Associating something pleasurable with an action that would otherwise cause concern will often overcome the problem, but beware of creating even greater problems. One dog I know who was slightly nervous of the gun was sent very quickly for birds that had been shot to make him forget his fear. Yes, he forgot his nervousness but now runs in to every shot he hears.

Overcoming gun nervousness can be time consuming, and requires a lot of patience, but when your dog looks knowingly at you as you appear with gun in slip and waits to join you for the shoot, you know you are getting there, and the work has been worth while.

If your dog is steady at a drive, you can concentrate on the shooting – once the drive is over, concentrate just as hard on your dog work. Make sure your dog does not play with or change birds when retrieving and, if you want to remain friends with fellow Guns, do not let him play with other dogs who are working, or, worse, take birds from their mouths.

A question I am often asked by Guns is, 'What do you do when all through the summer your dog has been doing everything perfectly but when you get into the field and on to the real thing, he runs riot?' This applies particularly to Guns since they are often in a situation where they cannot reach the dog to administer a correction.

I was picking up on one occasion when a friend came up to me and told me that his dog was on an island in the middle of the lake we had driven for duck; the dog had found a dead duck and was messing about with it. Neither demand nor threat could make her return with this retrieve. My suggestion that he should strip off and swim across to get into contact was not received with the humour that was intended. So we tried the next best thing, which was to walk away from the lake as though going back to the cars. Within seconds, the dog was back across from the island, duck in mouth and running after her handler. A little psychology had worked, but as this was the second time she had done it, how was he going to ensure that it would not happen again?

I really feel that the answer lies in correctly introducing the dog to the field to begin with, together with ensuring that he has had a thorough grounding in the basics, particularly the 'Stop' and 'Recall' whistle. If you cannot stop your dog at any time and get him back to you, start working at it.

There is no doubt that the company of friends at a shoot, and the shooting itself, not only takes your concentration from the dog, but also makes you embarrassed to do anything about a misdemeanour should it occur. The problem is that if you do not nip the fault in the bud at the moment it happens, the dog will not know that he has done something wrong. It has been suggested that you could simulate the same situation later using dummies or cold game but, in these circumstances, the dog will probably behave perfectly. The only way to get things right is to be a dog man first, especially in the early days. Keep an eye on your dog, read his mind and actions and be one step ahead.

There may be particular situations that are a signal for your dog to misbehave, but I wonder if your dog realizes that he is misbehaving. He may believe that he is doing the right thing because of what you have taught him to do before. Some dogs only run amok when the owner is actually shooting, gun in hand. Somewhere along the line, such a dog has been taught or allowed to do this, maybe even getting praised for it. The most obvious example is the Gun who brings down a bird which runs and, not wishing to lose it, sends the dog immediately. On return, the dog receives lavish praise from a proud owner, which reinforces the habit, and the dog's virtues are proudly extolled to all Guns present. Now the dog begins to associate gun, shot, retrieve – *praise*. If he is a young dog, he will not have associated praise with the fact that the bird was running. This association may come with an experienced dog as he gains in years and knowledge of what is required in each circumstance, but not in a youngster.

The character of a dog may exacerbate the problem: a dominant, even clever dog who is strong, resourceful and independent, will be especially difficult to correct once you have allowed the situation to arise. A strong-willed dog who ignores you in order to get a retrieve should certainly not be praised when he brings it to you; but can you punish him when he has returned with the prize? The answer has got to be 'no' unless he knows he has done something wrong and, particularly, *what* he has done wrong, otherwise he will associate the punishment with the return, not with the run in. You must, therefore, put yourself

in a position to stop the run in. The most obvious way is to tie your dog to the peg. I know it seems an admission of defeat, but if you do this and then walk around afterwards with dog at heel and pick the birds yourself, allowing the pickers-up to retrieve the difficult ones, he may start to get the message.

Gradually work away from his being tied up: to begin with, allow the lead to hang lose, and then just wrap it around his neck; next, lay it on the floor in front of the dog, and finally remove it altogether. This gradual process may be spread over a number of outings, depending on how the dog reacts. With a strong-willed dog, you will need to establish a high degree of discipline from the very beginning and if, at any stage, he begins to take advantage, go back to strict discipline training – sits, stays, temptations (but very little retrieving if any at all), and walking closely to heel – what you might call old-fashioned square bashing. With this type of dog, you know you are winning if, upon being given a command, he looks to you for reassurances that he is doing the right thing before obeying. When you tell him to jump, he does not do it without asking 'How high?'.

Other ways of dealing with the problem include removing the lead but attaching a light check cord that the dog may not notice. If the dog takes off, this will bring him up with a very sharp jolt – a strong reprimand. It is important to make sure that the cord is not so long that the dog gets up to top speed and then damages himself when he is stopped abruptly. However, some dogs will very quickly learn to know when they have the check cord on and when they are unfettered. You might also find that fellow Guns find this a source of great amusement.

The electronic collar is a possibility

and, although I do not advocate its use nor use it myself as a normal training aid, there are times when it can be very advantageous: the problem we are discussing here could be one of them. When a dog thinks that you cannot get into contact with him and so does his own thing, it would come as quite a shock (pun intended) if you could reinforce your command with a mild punishment and catch him in the act. There have been dogs brought to me for rehabilitation who could have benefited from such a device.

The real answer is not to scrimp on your basic training and to go intently through all the stages of development while realizing that training never stops. Just because your dog will sit to a thrown dummy, a dummy launcher and even birds that others have shot, you cannot be lulled into the false feeling of security that everything else will fall into place. Some dogs are more difficult than others and some will take advantage no matter how much you try. They are either stronger willed than you or the temptation is much greater than either their respect for you or fear of retribution. Some dogs are just impossible – but do not think that yours is one of these and make excuses for your own failings. Create training exercises and situations that will enable you to get on top of your dog and ensure he obeys your commands. There are no quick and easy answers.

Take pride in your dog work and if both of you have done your homework well, you will be surprised how much enjoyment you will get from it. Many Guns have told me that after discovering what it is to work a good dog, they often prefer working the dog to shooting.

8 The Rough Shooter's Dog

How often do you hear the statement, 'I don't want anything special – he will only be for rough shooting', used as an excuse for not bringing a dog up to an acceptable standard? Or, even worse, the handler who admits to tolerating unsteadiness in his dog because he is only used for rough shooting. Why is rough shooting considered so lowly that any old mutt, without even the simplest form of training, will suffice to do the job? It would seem that as long as the dog roots about and pushes up the odd head of game or a rabbit which may present itself in such a way that it can be shot, that should be enough. It may be because the rough shooter is usually out on his own, or with only one or two friends who have similar dogs, that the acceptance of poor standards has come about. No one notices how bad a dog is and, because he is by himself, no one is offended.

A dog is out with a gun to put game into the bag and, in order to maximize the opportunities of doing this, he has to be skilful and efficient. The dog who does not

An informal rough shoot can be a rewarding day with good dogs.

hunt his ground well and methodically, could miss the game that will give the Gun a shot. On a rough shoot, the game is often very thin on the ground, so good hunting is essential if you are to get a shot. A dog who chases a rabbit may deny the Gun the chance of a shot by being in between the Gun and the rabbit. The dog who runs in to the shot can flush game while the gun is unloaded, and shot game can be left unrecovered if the dog is a poor retriever. These are just a few of the faults that shooters are prepared to put up with on the basis that all they do is rough shooting.

Rough shooting is real dog work: it takes us back to the times when man was a hunter, and the aim was to put food on the table. I particularly enjoy rough shooting where, in the company of a good dog, I search for that elusive quarry, which once shot and in the bag, provides me with the satisfaction of knowing that we could provide food for the family. Old-fashioned maybe, but to come back at the end of the day with a variety of game, albeit small in number, shows that my dog and I have the skills to find, shoot and bring back the sustenance that life demands. To do this, a rough-shooting dog has to be not only Jack of all trades but master of many.

For a dog, a day's work may involve hunting cover, sitting in woods waiting for roosting pigeon, swimming to retrieve wildfowl, walking to heel or waiting patiently out of sight while you stalk a rabbit around a corner, finding that difficult dead bird or runner that you know you hit, and doing these and many other skilled jobs. Also, he must work with the minimum of noise and disturbance since

The ideal rough-shooter's dog – the English Springer Spaniel (note the kind, honest eye of this particular dog).

Watch your dog and read the signals he gives you. He should always work within shooting distance to give you the chance of a shot.

A dog who sits to flush is safe and you can concentrate on the shot.

A good delivery right up to hand completes the thrill of good hunting, successful shot and retrieve. A good rough-shooting dog should be a dog to be proud of.

noise will make the few head of game present on the rough shoot quickly disappear. In my opinion, the rough-shoot dog is the cream of the gundog world and deserves to be trained to a high standard, not only to give you the shooting and birds in the bag, but also to enhance your day. If you have a good, working companion in front of you who gives you pleasurable moments within the day, it can only improve the quality of your shooting days.

The ideal rough-shooting dog is usually imagined to be the English Springer but as long as you have a dog who will work any type of cover under control it does not really matter. I have a number of friends who rough shoot with retrievers and continental HPRs (Hunt, Point, Retrieve). They find that the dogs match their own temperament, character and individual needs so this becomes their

preference. No matter what the dog, he has to hunt and flush like a spaniel, retrieve and handle like a retriever; and if he points like a pointer, to give you the chance to prepare yourself for the shot, then even better. To do all this, the rough shooter's dog needs a comprehensive training programme which will develop the skills that he is likely to need in the field. All aspects of such a training programme have been covered in this and my previous book, *Working Gundogs*. To my mind, there are no special requirements, just the potential to handle any type of work or situation that may arise.

I feel that the rough-shooting dog's status should be raised to a point where one is proud to say: 'He is a rough-shooting dog'. A well-trained dog under control makes your shooting days so much more enjoyable, and you do not need to end the day exasperated and hoarse.

9 The Wildfowler's Dog

The toughest shooting in many ways is wildfowling. Out in the early morning or late afternoon on cold winter days, the wildfowler sees Mother Nature in all her glory on the marshes and saltings, and waits for the opportunity to reap a small harvest of duck or geese. Cold, often wet, his dog will be expected to sit patiently and quietly until galvanized into action by the sound of wings, the call of the fowl, the shot from the gun, the fall of the bird and then the command to retrieve. Strong tides, thick mud and silt, heavy reeds and extreme cold can all be present to hinder the successful retrieve, but the good wildfowler's dog will have a determination to succeed that is almost a fanaticism. Many wildfowlers choose their dogs from lines that have this daredevil commando approach. They work on their own, as independent and confident of their own ability as their master, and do not know the meaning of the word failure. Although this high degree of initiative and drive is an essential characteristic of the wildfowler's dog, he must also be well trained and controlled if the wildfowler is to enjoy his sport and help the dog to do his work.

A wildfowler without a dog runs the risk of losing birds in the darkness, on moving water or where a strong wind can carry them away, particularly when the birds are runners or divers. The use of a dog shows a respect for the quarry and a determination to put shot birds in the bag.

The most popular breed for this work is undoubtedly the Labrador Retriever whose thick, oily coat provides an insulated, waterproof covering to protect him from the elements. Chesapeake Bay Retrievers are also strong water dogs, but you must ensure that you get a dog from a good working line of the breed to be confident of their potential for training and natural ability for shooting. Golden Retrievers are occasionally used, as are Springer Spaniels and even Cocker Spaniels, but, in my opinion, the spaniel breeds generally do not possess the strength and weatherproofing of the retriever breeds. In the cold weather, after a few swims, the spaniel will feel the cold as the water permeates his coat. I have used spaniels wildfowling, and they certainly look wretched very quickly: even covering them with a sack or other warm material appears to do little to alleviate their suffering. Being short of leg they also find the natural terrain of the marshes difficult to deal with. These dogs are more suited to bustling and busting the bramble, bracken and gorse patches of rough woodland.

Having said that, I know many wildfowlers who favour spaniels and one fenshooter friend of mine tells me that, in his opinion, his Springer swims in the dykes and in the sea better than a Labrador because his body is smaller, so he swims

Some wildfowlers prefer spaniels.

closer to the surface of the water and thus is not held back by the drag of current under the surface. The parti-coloured coat, liver and white or black and white, provides a better camouflage against a background of mud and water, and his particular dogs did not mind the cold. It just goes to prove that there are no hard and fast rules: you must look for and work with a dog who appeals to you and who does the job well.

Whatever breed you decide on, if the dog's main work is to be wildfowling, look for one that not only has a personality that meets your own likes, but also one that will have the build and character required to do the job. The working Labrador, for example, comes in many shapes and sizes, and it is worth doing a little homework to ensure that when your pup grows into adulthood, he will meet your needs. It may be that the well-known field trial and working dogs of the

day are too small to meet the challenge of your sport. Even though they have the drive and ability, they may be lacking in raw strength. Talk to other wildfowlers, get to know their dogs and their background and seek out the ideal dog for you.

Working mainly in water and in semi- or even complete darkness, the wildfowler's dog needs to be trained and given experience to handle these situations. Sometimes he will be expected to hunt reeds on the opposite bank of a river or gully, while at other times he will be asked to range far and wide, often getting out a considerable distance on water or land to bring off the retrieve. He may have to cross more than one creek, river or stream to reach the fall area, and then to work completely unbidden to find the bird. The bird may range in size from the small, such as a teal, to a large goose. A large goose can be a considerable burden

A large goose can be quite a burden for a dog.

if it has to be brought back against the tide or carried over the mud, testing the dog's strength and stamina. The teal may create few problems in being carried, but may need more experience of nose-work to locate.

Prior to being galvanized into action, the dog can be sitting for considerable periods of time. He must wait quietly: fidgeting can easily distract the fowler and may even bring his presence to the attention of approaching fowl. Patience (sitting and waiting) training can be carried out at any time, and is a desirable skill in many working situations, but it is worth spending time with the dog developing some of the additional skills he will require to enhance the basic training you have carried out.

During his basic training, your dog will have developed the ability to mark the fall of a bird by sight. If he is to work in poor light, it is essential that he also develops the ability to mark the fall by sound. The most obvious way of doing this is to take your dog out when it is dark and do some retrieving training. It will be more useful to the dog if the dummies are thrown by someone other than yourself as the dog will see the direction of the throw if you do it yourself. An assistant, out of sight, can launch a dummy at the sound of a shot from yourself. The dog, hearing the sound of the fall, can then be sent. Initially, do not make the retrieves too difficult, so that the dog quickly succeeds when he follows the direction signal you have given as you send him. The sound of the fall and the direction given by your hand will build your dog's confidence which can lead you to reducing the sound of the fall gradually as it gets more distant, or even having no sound at all and the dog taking direction solely from your hand. You must realize that in the dark you will not be able to see

113

An experienced Golden Retriever teaching a young recruit all about swimming – one of the few instances where I would use an older dog to help teach a young one.

If you are a coastal wildfowler, make sure your dog has had experience in the sea.

when your dog is in the right area of the fall (even if you knew where that was) to give him the command to hunt.

A dog with a natural quartering action that he brings into play when he thinks he is in the right area is very advantageous. The dog who hunts his ground naturally and works systematically for the retrieve is more likely to succeed than one who looks to you for instruction and, when not getting any because you cannot see him, runs around aimlessly. Hiding dummies or throwing small balls in heavy cover and then encouraging a dog to hunt without giving any guidance, will help him to develop this skill. Keep him hunting in the fall area and, if he is a dog who naturally sticks to the fall of the retrieve, let him work it on his own until successful. If he is not a natural, develop this skill by encouraging him back to the fall area and keeping him hunting until successful.

Some dogs have natural hunting and working patterns, which are an advantage; others, of course, have to develop them as they are trained. Watch your dog through all his stages of training and work at bringing out the style of work which will benefit your type of fowling.

In addition to advanced water work, it has to be worth while to stretch the dog's experience of the various environments he will encounter. Marshes and saltings with reed beds, creeks and gullies are very different to the pleasant lake and stream of the countryside, so spend time doing training exercises in this setting. Train your dog at night-time on water, again developing his ability to mark by sound as a dummy splashes into the water or on to a far bank. For this, the dummy launcher can be a useful piece of equipment, propelling a dummy for a considerable distance on to or over water.

Many wildfowlers prefer a dog who runs into the fall of a shot bird. This is because the dog has a better chance of retrieving the bird before the current or tide sweeps it away or, if it is a runner, before it manages to put distance between itself and you. The problem with allowing your dog to do this is that you will develop a dog who will continue to run in at any type of shoot and, although it does not create any concern when you are by yourself, it can be an embarrassment at formal shoots. It is debatable, however, whether a dog running in to the fall and, ultimately, the shot, has an advantage. A dog who leaves the starting blocks immediately a shot is fired often has more difficulty marking the fall and, believing that he knows better than you, will generally ignore any assistance. It must also be considered that a duck that falls into the water may be washed ashore by tide or wind, sparing the dog a very cold swim and sitting about getting even colder afterwards. A dog who runs in to the fall can alarm other approaching birds and cause them to avoid your position. In addition, if you use decoys, a dog who runs in out of control can easily become entangled in the lines holding them.

I would recommend that any shooter, including the wildfowler, maintains steadiness in his dog at all times. If you have a steady dog who only moves for a retrieve on command, you are retaining that essential control. You can speed up the command if the duck is a runner, or make the dog wait until the retrieve can be carried out at a more convenient moment. The important thing is that the decision is yours, and your dog waits until you make it. You will find that by doing this you will not only avoid a lot of frustration and annoyance, but you

Creeping up to a creek. A dog who runs in may have to be put on the lead. This makes the work harder and could be dangerous for both dog and Gun.

will also minimize the possibility of putting your dog and even yourself into a difficult, maybe even dangerous position.

DIVERS

The handling of divers comes with experience, and it is difficult to provide training exercises which will simulate this. A strong, diving duck is a very difficult retrieve as it can surface anywhere, sometimes even in reeds where it is not seen. Ducks have the ability to stay underwater for a considerable time, and when they surface are often difficult to spot as they put their heads low along the top of the water and paddle very smoothly and quickly away from a searching dog. A swimming dog will have difficulty seeing the bird, and should therefore be well schooled in taking hand signals from you. Some dogs develop very skilful methods of dealing with divers, and develop a knack of knowing where they will surface, consistently following the duck until it tires and they can then catch it. One of my spaniels developed the ability to swim underwater following a diving duck and catching it below the surface. I have known other dogs who do this and many who become skilful at putting their heads just below the surface of the water as the duck dives, catching it at that moment.

Most wounded duck will swim to shore where, if they then tuck in among the reeds or other undergrowth, they will be more easily located and caught. A dog who effectively hunts the vegetation alongside land, by entering the water to hunt the marginal vegetation and then coming ashore to hunt the land vegetation, is going to have more chance of success. If your dog is under control, has

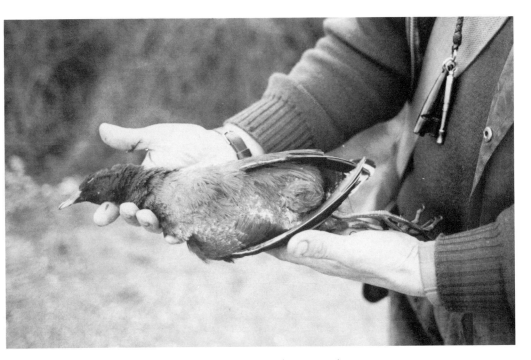

A moorhen is a good first retrieve for any dog because of its size and tight feathers.

been taught to hunt and will stop to shot or the whistle, you can teach him to do this by hunting him spaniel-fashion amongst the vegetation after hiding dummies both in the water plants and on the banks. Occasionally, a shot can be fired and a dummy thrown ahead into the water or, better still, if there are moorhens these can be shot (in season) to give a retrieve on the real thing. By the way, do not waste the moorhen – it makes good eating.

Sometimes it may help to put a second shot into a wounded duck, but make sure that this is done safely. Shot can ricochet off water and travel a considerable distance, so make sure that your dog and other people are not in the vicinity of the shot. If your dog is young and inexperienced, a diver can create all types of problems. Therefore, if you can shoot it, do so, particularly if it is likely to escape capture otherwise, or if the conditions

make it a difficult retrieve where the dog may fail and lose confidence.

OUT IN THE COLD

Wildfowling can be an extremely cold pastime, and a swim in icy waters followed by a long wait in a cold wind can be very uncomfortable for your dog. Enthusiastic though your dog may be, he will still feel the cold even if he does not seem to take much notice of it. Frequent dips in sub-zero waters accelerate the onset of arthritis and rheumatism, reducing your dog's active working years and comfortable life. A little thought can reduce the possibility of health problems. Wind increases the cooling effect, so, if you can, protect your dog from the wind by covering him in a windproof material. I have found that an old wax-proofed jacket or a piece of canvas

117

A loner's sport. A wildfowler and his dog wait hopefully for birds to flight up a creek.

towelling down is not required. If you do ever towel your dog, do not rub up and down the coat, but only in a downward direction with the lie of the coat. Vigorous rubbing backwards and forwards pushes water into the base of the coat and into the skin where the cold then penetrates even more. So let the dog shake well, keep the wind off him and, when you have finished shooting and are back at the car, towel your dog off and put him into a drying bag made of soft hessian or thick towelling. You can buy commercial versions of these bags, but it is just as easy to make them. The bag should enclose all the body of your dog up to the neck where it is fastened by zipper, poppers or draw cord. Most dogs quickly accept this comfortable garment and, once in it, settle down happily for the journey home. Upon reaching home, their own body heat held within the bag will have dried them, and any dirt will have fallen off into the bag where it can easily be shaken out or washed. An added advantage is that your car stays cleaner.

Your dog may have to travel by boat. Here a Golden Retriever, Labrador and Curly Coated Retriever share transport.

thrown over the dog's back often provides the necessary protection. An old hessian sack, slit up one side, with a hole cut in the bottom corner and placed over the dog in the form of a poncho keeps out the wind and also retains the dog's body heat, helping him to dry out more quickly – this type of garment is not advised if your dog runs in, for obvious reasons!

After a swim, your dog will shake to rid himself of surplus water and, usually,

Wildfowling is very much a loner's sport, where the dog provides the most rewarding form of companionship. A dog who is under control, working with you in closeness and friendship to complete the retrieves, adds a new dimension to the sport and to the meaning of man/dog relationships.

10   The Pigeon Shooter's Dog

Pigeon shooting can offer one of the most enjoyable days for any shooting man. For me, actually to bring down one of these wily quarries, is a feat in itself. I have found – and I am not an expert pigeon shooter – that the secret lies not only in finding flight lines, feed areas and setting out a good decoy pattern, but also in good camouflage and the ability to keep very still. The flutter of an eyelash, and these very observant birds are heading in the opposite direction, so a dog who is always demanding attention can spoil your whole day. The movements you make in attempting to keep some semblance of control and discipline will surely be noticed by the most short-sighted of pigeons.

Basically, there are two types of pigeon shooting: roost shooting and decoying, and there is no doubt that the partnership of a good dog can enhance either of these particularly enjoyable pastimes. The emphasis, though, has got to be on 'a good dog'. For some reason, pigeon shooting is considered a down-market sport, the working man's game and, without really considering the facts, many shooters have the impression that a pigeon-shooting dog need not be one who is highly trained or of a particularly good working strain. Nothing could be further from the truth.

Roost shooting is probably the easier of the two to train the dog to work on, as it is very similar to a formal shoot day. The dog sits and waits until sent by the handler for a bird that has been shot. The shooter who works over decoys, however, has added complications. Sitting in a hide, the dog may not see the fall of a bird and, when sent, has to negotiate this obstruction before getting out into the field where he is faced with plastic and, more often, real bird decoys as well as the one he has been sent for – which one does he retrieve?

The training of a good pigeon dog follows the same lines as any other training regime for a gundog. He must learn to be steady and patient, sitting quietly and waiting for the handler's command. Some days, you may be sitting in the hide for a number of hours with only the occasional shot and even less to retrieve; if you have a relaxed dog you can become a relaxed shooter. This is probably the reason why most pigeon-shooting men prefer a retriever, which by nature tends to be more placid than a spaniel. Take your time teaching the dog to sit and stay, and practise going out of sight for a considerable period of time. There will be occasions when you will want your dog to wait by himself while you set up the hide, and you will certainly not be popular if your dog is hunting the hedgerows while you are doing this, particularly if game birds are nesting. The dog will have to wait in the hide for the birds to arrive or for you

Roost shooting. Your dog will have to be steady and able to mark the fall.

to put out the decoys. Training your dog to sit calmly for long periods often develops a more relaxed dog, and the habit he learns of 'slipping into neutral' will pay dividends many times over.

To ensure that your dog is not free-hunting you must always be aware of where your dog is. For this he should be a reliable 'heeler'. Carrying a lot of pigeon-shooting kit requires your hands to be used for things other than holding a lead, so a dog who walks to heel without a lead on the way to the shoot area makes your task much easier.

The dog should be able to take directions and particularly understand the word 'No', which is often used initially to tell the dog that the bird he is considering bringing back is not the one you want. He should have been carefully and completely introduced to gunfire, including shots fired in the confines of a hide. A shot fired in the hide, the straw-bale type in particular, can create a very disturbing sound to a young dog; and even though he may not appear to be gun-shy, a considerable amount of shooting done over a young dog in a hide can easily create a sensitivity to shot.

Introduction to feather may not always be easy. The pigeon has a very strong scent and the feathers are extremely loose, and some young dogs find them distasteful. The best way to introduce your dog to pigeon is to wrap a dead one in a nylon stocking and use this for retrieves, gradually reducing the amount of stocking around the bird by cutting holes to allow the head to poke out and then the wings until finally your dog is retrieving the undisguised bird. Always remember to wipe the feathers out of your dog's mouth with your hand. Freshly shot birds lose their feathers very easily, and a mouthful of these must be very uncomfortable. A dog

who retrieves a lot of birds will in fact swallow a considerable number of feathers, and a useful tip is to give your dog a good spoonful of cod-liver oil once a week during heavy shooting to help clear out what could otherwise cause a considerable blockage.

As well as the basics, teach your dog to 'Get Out' and take hand signals, sending him to the left or right. These, coupled with the word 'No', as previously mentioned, will quickly teach your dog to look to you and take directions to the bird you require. A dog who has all the natural instincts and interest in the shooting life will often go for the moving bird anyway, as this is the one that will catch his eye. However, there will be times when the bird is hidden from view and you will want to get the dog into the right area for the retrieve without leaving your hide, hence the importance of hand signals. A good pigeon dog should use his initiative and work virtually unaided once he has been trained and gained experience, and so there has to be a careful balance in training between control, to achieve the required results, and allowing your dog to work freely, so that he can use his own instinct and natural hunting drive.

On the way out to the retrieve, your dog will have to ignore decoy pigeons; often these are birds which have been shot only minutes before and then placed within the pattern. To help you achieve this, throw multiple dummies and train your dog to fetch only the one that you direct him on to. Put dummies in line, stopping the dog just before he gets to the first one and sending him on to the second, further away. Introduce distractions: as the dog returns with a dummy, throw another over his head to simulate a shot bird — encourage the dog to ignore this and bring you the one in his mouth first. With

The pigeon shooter's dog will have to learn to pick freshly shot birds from amongst decoys.

dummies, simulate as many situations as may possibly occur on a shooting foray.

Once you have built the basic obedience and discipline into your dog, introduced him to gunfire and accustomed him to hearing this in enclosed spaces, and familiarized him with feather, there is then the most important part of the training left: experience – learning through doing the real thing. Your dog will never stop learning. A young dog appears to learn quickly, but only because there is such a lot to learn when you know very little. As the dog gets older, you can polish the performance, adding small refinements that will make your day more pleasurable and also create that special bond between you and your dog. By sending your dog for the freshly shot runners, he will learn to look for movement the moment he leaves the hide. Take care, however, not to create a running-in problem, as this can easily occur. If there is no movement and the dog

realizes that you are not sending him for an unseen, he will learn to search amongst the decoys for the one you require. He may begin to notice that the bird you are asking for is the one on its back and not the one with the stick stuck under the chin holding the head up or, more particularly, the bird you want does not have your hand's scent on it.

I remember at a cold-game test, one competitor who was running his dog for the first time in such an event. Not fully realizing what was involved, he explained that he had a problem as his dog would not touch game that had human scent on it. The dog had been used for pigeon shooting and picking up, and had been taught not to pick game that was soiled in this way. He was right to be concerned – his dog found the game in the test, looked at him and then came directly back, leaving the bird or rabbit where it originally lay.

Your dog should be in a position to get a good view of the 'drop' area.

Make sure there is a clear exit . . .

An impetuous dog who may run in can cause total chaos in a net hide. It is quite a good idea to build a hide so that both you and your dog can keep an eye on proceedings. With a net hide you can both look through the netting. Perched on your drum, you can then, from a sitting position, raise your gun above the level of the hide and shoot the pigeon dropping in on your decoys. The dog, looking through the netting, sees this tempting picture of a falling bird, forgets the net and takes off with net, poles and cursing handler following behind. So train your dog to wait until you have lifted a corner of the hide for him to exit; when you lift the corner, make him wait a few extra seconds before sending him, otherwise the time will come when you will not be able to raise the corner quickly enough!

Most dogs will leave the hide and return through the same place. Unfortunately, they are not always consistent in their choice of place, so the more controlled your dog is at this lifting of the curtain, the less chance there is of your having to rebuild your hide. Depending on the background cover and the wariness of the pigeons, you can sometimes dispense with the front of the hide or have a large gap at the bottom.

If you are right-handed, sit your dog on the right-hand side — if left-handed, on your left. The reason for this is that when you have taken a shot you will break your gun. If you are right-handed, you will do so over your left knee. In the event of an accidental discharge, and it does happen,

. . . and entrance on return.

you will only end up with a hole in the hide, not in your dog.

Some dogs become experienced very quickly, others take longer and need careful, firm handling. No dog is the same. With experience, some dogs can learn some very useful tricks. The late and much respected guru of pigeon shooting, Archie Coates, used to recount the story of his old dog whom he had taught to drop a pigeon on its breast, not its back, and in the right spot amongst the decoys. To get him to drop the right way up was not easy but, when a bird had been dropped on its back by mistake one day and the dog looked at Archie before calmly turning it over with his foot so that it lay in the correct manner, Archie knew that the dog fully understood what was required. For me, that moment of partnership, and also amusement, would have given far more pleasure than shooting any bird.

In general, a dog will not have received enough training or become mature enough to work effectively with a pigeon shooter until he is about eighteen months to two years old. If you can work him with an older dog during the early stages, this can be beneficial, providing the old dog teaches the young one the right tricks.

In addition to firing shots at pigeon flighting in, the experienced pigeon shooter will often fire scaring shots to get the pigeon moving. When this happens, the dog should learn to relax and remain in neutral. You will be surprised how quickly he will get to know when you are shooting to kill and when you are shooting to scare, from the posture you adopt. You will also be surprised how quickly the dog gets to know when you have missed from the words that you use – or, at least, your tone of voice. 'Gone Away' will suffice to let your dog know there is nothing to fetch.

When decoying over laid corn, wait until the birds are well in so that you can drop them close to the hide on the laid area. This shows respect for the farmer and his standing crop, and also for your quarry. Shooting a bird far out so that it is wounded and falls into standing corn leaves you in a bit of a dilemma. Do you have respect for your quarry and send your dog to retrieve it? Or do you have respect for the farmer and his crop, which could be damaged to an even greater extent by your dog searching for the bird? If you shoot sensibly this situation should rarely occur.

One final thought, which has little to do with training, but a lot to do with the relationship and understanding which you build up with your dog. Sitting in a hide, with numerous shots being fired over him, can create deafness in your dog. Learn to notice when the deafness is real. Even when a dog has had his hearing affected by gunfire, he will usually hear a whistle command, even though he has problems with verbal ones. You should have trained your dog to the whistle anyway, but this is an additional benefit from doing so.

With good training and experience, the pigeon shooter and his dog can become a team. The dog will know what is required, working with the minimum of commands while the shooter gets on with his job. Effort and preparation, together with experience, will help you get the most from your dog; and it is your dog's work which, many times, will provide the highlight of your day.

11 Gundog Tests and Other Competitions

At some time, most gundog owners are tempted to run their dog in some form of competition. For many, this may be an informal type of test such as those regularly run at many small game or country fairs. Some tests are mainly for fun, to create an interest for spectators and dog owner alike. The Scurry and Pick-Up are two such tests that are based on practical work, and with the emphasis on speed of dog work. A more formal test, the Working test, has become very popular and now has a considerable number of devotees who will travel great distances to work their dogs in them.

THE SCURRY

The Scurry is probably the test that requires the least skills of all on the part of the handler and dog. If you have a fast dog who marks well and returns speedily to hand, this could be the test for you. As with all tests, the way the Scurry is operated depends upon the organizer. In most cases, the dog is sat behind a line and one or two seen retrieves are thrown or launched from a dummy launcher. These retrieves can be on land or water, or both, and in various covers. Once the retrieves have been thrown, you will be given the 'Start' command, and the moment your dog crosses the line, the stop watch will be started. The watch is stopped and the

time that has been taken read off when your dog recrosses the line with the last retrieve. In some Scurries you will be told in which order the dummies are to be retrieved, and the watch may be stopped only when the last dummy is in your hand. I personally prefer the watch being stopped when the dog crosses the line, otherwise, in his haste, the handler will be grabbing at the dog and dummy which could cause problems.

The dog with the fastest time at the end of the day wins. In most Scurries, handling is very limited. In fact, if you have to handle or direct your dog, you will be taking longer to do the retrieve and your time will be poor.

THE PICK-UP

Based on the work of picking up, the Pick-Up test simulates such situations where there are a number of birds down that you and your dog have not seen. Again, the test is against the clock and you and your dog work to pick up the dummies in the fastest time. Usually, there will be about five dummies down and you will be given a time limit. If you take longer than this, the number of dummies picked is counted; if you pick up all the dummies within the time limit, the time is counted.

To be successful in a Pick-Up test, your

127

dog will have to go out promptly for an unseen dummy, hunt briskly and purposefully, stop on the whistle and take directions. All this will have to be done at a good pace to achieve a winning time. In addition, your dog must accept the fact that there is more than one dummy to be picked. Many dogs will relax or give up after retrieving one or two dummies, as they have never picked more than that in previous exercises.

Both Scurries and Pick-Ups are competitions that should be taken lightly, with the aim of having a little fun with your dog. As they are against the clock, the pressure of time can make you behave in a completely different way to normal. Shouting, grabbing dummies, exciting or frightening the dog and letting good habits slip are only some of the errors caused by these competitions. I certainly would not run a young, inexperienced dog in such a competition unless it was for fun and I did all parts of the retrieving exercises properly, with no concern for time. When I have run such tests, there are always a number of owners who do just this – they enter to run their dog as part of the day's enjoyment and, not wanting to spoil their dog in any way, they pay no heed to the timing and speed of work. Know your dog and your own ability when you enter these competitions, and beware of causing problems for yourself and your dog through a few seconds of thoughtlessness. It is so easy in these competitions to create running in, a noisy dog and poor delivery, and these faults are only for starters!

WORKING TESTS

The growth in the popularity of Working tests for gundogs has been rapid, resulting now in national tests, such as those

Gundog tests have become quite prestigious events. The captains of the international teams receiving their awards at the CLA Game Fair at Stratfield Saye.

run at the Country Landowners Association Game Fair, which are quite prestigious. Most gundog associations run tests as well as trials. Some associations will run only tests. The original idea of the gundog test was to measure the progress of the dog and handler on their way to practical work in the field and at trials, and was organized for members attending training classes. For most, the test was not to assess performance at the end of training but to assess progress in order to help the handler to identify problem areas and weaknesses in the dog's training. They were often run at the end of a session of training or upon completion of the summer season's training classes. However, the interest in training a dog to work, and the competitive spirit in humans, has created an enthusiasm and interest in running the test as an end in itself. Some handlers never go further than running in tests, and their dogs may never have picked warm game. In some cases, they may not even have picked cold game.

This is not a criticism, just a statement of fact, but it does concern me that the test may become so influential a part of the gundog world that a dog may be bred from and puppies selected on the basis of test results alone. If this does become the case, people buying such dogs must be aware of their background and their possible limitations. When the precise location of a dummy is known, either seen or unseen, there is a tendency to over-handle to help the dog to the exact position. The dogs who will do well could therefore be those who do not possess hunting initiative and drive, but the ability to respond to directions alone.

The American retriever trials are run on similar lines to our tests, using live game but with dead retrieves falling in the same place. Dogs are trained and expected to run long straight lines without deviation, and depend upon their handlers rather than their own ability to find the game. The result has been that they have some good 'guided missiles' but poor hunters. These dogs seriously lack the abilities required by the normal shooting man.

To train the dogs to handle as automatons, forced techniques have been used: electronic collars, to shock them when they are doing the wrong thing; and check or guiding cords to channel all their movements in the direction required by the handler. One American trainer told me that he always force-retrieved his dogs, as this was the only way to get a reliable retriever and, if the dog was too sensitive to take the electronic collar, he was no use to him. The dog resulting from this training and breeding regime is hard in temperament and far removed from the true working dog that is required in the field. Many American trainers are now approaching the training of their dogs based on the British methods, and are using British bloodlines to bring back some of the natural abilities and characteristics which they have lost. My concern is that if the tests become very popular and an end in themselves, we may end up with dogs that are good at tests and win them, but are not of the type needed for true shooting work. There should not be a distinction between a test gundog and a shooting-field gundog.

A test is carried out using dummies or cold game. The majority use dummies of the canvas type. A number of exercises are set and each dog attempts exactly the same exercise with dummies being placed or thrown in the same location. By using dummies and placing them in exactly the same spot each time, the dog is not being tested on all the qualities necessary to make a good gundog. Hard-mouth cannot be tested with dummies, although I did judge one test where this was attempted by putting eggs in the dummy which the dog carried. If the eggs were broken, the dog was given no points. However, I have known dogs who will carry dummies – and eggs – perfectly, but bite game. I have to add that I have also known dogs who bite and mouth dummies but handle game very gently, so the egg test is not always conclusive.

Giving tongue or whining (another serious fault) at a test is rare because the excitement and temptation of warm game is not present, and so this particularly annoying and unwanted habit, again, cannot be tested. In fact, because there is no game scent or live game, the dogs are not open to the ultimate temptations that have to be controlled and channelled during the real thing. Dogs who retrieve dummies do not automatically retrieve game. I have also found, while watching many tests, that the dogs running lower down the running order follow the foot scent taken by previous dogs to help them to locate a dummy. This is only one example of a dog who has become test-wise. On hidden retrieves, I have seen experienced test dogs looking intently for the dummy placer.

One of the prime requirements of a gundog is game-finding ability. Dummy-finding ability and tracking human and other dogs' scent does not prove that he has this game-finding ability. It is easy to identify the spaniel who has become test-wise. He will quarter his ground with head held high all the time, bouncing over the cover and watching gun and dummy thrower for any sign of movement that will indicate the start of a retrieve. The moment the gun is raised or a hand

holding a dummy prepares to throw, the dog stops and watches, waiting for what he knows is to follow. This 'stickiness' and test awareness is not what we require, and the only way to overcome or avoid such a problem is not to over-test or over-use dummies with such a dog, but to give him plenty of real hunting work. The difference in the skills required for tests and for fieldwork must be taken into account, and winners of tests put into perspective against what we really require of a gundog.

Having said all that, there is no doubt that tests are enjoyable for handler and dog, and are a good way of measuring progress. They are also more of a spectator sport than trials because they do not use live game and can be staged where they can be more easily watched. Not only do they entertain others, but they also create an interest and understanding of our sport and ultimately, I hope, shooting. I also have to add that many dogs of today who do well in tests do equally well in trials and the shooting field, but this has been because in the preparation of a dog, the emphasis has been on shooting and not purely on tests.

The test will also give the handler experience of running in competitions, which, if the bug bites, can lead to field trials. Should this be where your interest lies, make sure that you understand the differences between tests and trials. In particular, if you are intending to enter trials, make sure that your dog does not exhibit any of the eliminating faults and has had experience of live game. If you are uncertain in any way, ask someone who trials regularly for their advice and opinion of you and your dog.

It is far easier to obtain a run in tests than in trials, and many associations organize their tests in such a way that anyone entering gets a run. Where there are a lot of entries, the format of the test may change to accommodate them all. In retriever tests, for example, three or four judges may be invited, and each judge asked to mark just one of the exercises.

Tests are not governed by the same rules and regulations that control field trials, but the judges are often experienced field triallers who know what is required from a good gundog and endeavour, under the constraints of test conditions, to test for those qualities.

Tests are organized by associations for their members who, at the beginning of the year, are sent a programme of tests to be run. Gundog associations will accept membership from anyone wishing to run in their tests or attend training classes, so you could join associations all over the country if you so wished.

There are four basic grades of test which can be run for retrievers – Puppy, Novice, Intermediate and Open; and Novice and Open for spaniels. A puppy is a dog who is under two years old on the date of the test, and Puppy tests are usually run in conjunction with Novice tests. Intermediate tests are not run by every association as they are often considered to be just a way of increasing the number of competitions that dogs can run in. The original idea of an Intermediate test, however, was to give dogs who had won Novice tests a half-way house before going on to compete in Open tests, which can be considerably more difficult. Because the rules governing many association's tests are informal, it is often left to the judgement of the handler to decide which test to enter. A dog who has won a Novice test or higher, or taken awards in field trials, cannot enter a Novice test, but many novice dogs do enter and run in Open tests without going through the

Novice, and Intermediate stages. The organizers of the tests decide whether they will allow them to run.

To enter a test, an entry form has to be completed which includes details of dog and handler. This is sent to the organizer with the respective entry fee before the closing date. The organizer will draw the running order on a stated day and inform all members who have entered of their running number.

The administration of a test follows similar lines to that of a trial, and the guide-lines mentioned in Chapter 12 are relevant to tests. Although associations differ in their organization of a test, there are generally two judges who will judge some tests either together or separately, depending on the type of test. In the event of a run off, the judges will judge together and compare notes and opinions.

A test is judged on a points basis, with a number of points being allocated to each individual test or exercise. This differs from trials where the judges grade the dog on an alphabetical scale, A, B, C, etc. with an additional plus or minus where necessary. The points are awarded according to the way you and your dog approach and handle the exercise. Just because you are successful at getting a retrieve does not mean that you will get maximum points. How you did it, how much whistle and command were necessary, the way in which the dog worked and his style are some of the factors that the judge will consider in awarding points.

Whether you are hunting a spaniel or attempting a retrieve, the judge is looking for the ability to handle the situation. The good handlers and dogs make an exercise look easy, with the minimum of fuss and noise. A lot of whistling and shouting will lose you points. A dog who has to be handled on to a seen retrieve will lose points. If you have to walk forward to help your dog, you will lose points. You will lose a lot of points if your dog commits some of the major faults such as swapping dummies, running out of control, dropping the dummy and, particularly, running in to a thrown dummy. You may even be eliminated from that test with no points.

You should know your dog and his ability: do not enter tests until you feel that he has reached the required standard. Good tests are well designed to create a challenge for you and your dog, but you should feel confident that you can succeed at them with taught skills, natural ability and effort. Tests are to measure your progress and they are fun, so I would encourage you to enter them and to measure your performance yourself, and to learn by it what to do next with you dog.

Because of the informality and social aspects of a test, some handlers enter their dogs too early and, in doing so, create problems for themselves and their dogs, which are difficult to overcome. A test puts you in a situation where you are being watched by others in a competitive position; this can cause nerves and stress, which does not aid rational thought and action when you get into difficulties. A young dog needs to succeed quickly to progress, and I have seen handlers working their dogs for too long on an unseen retrieve that was too difficult for them and was, in the end, demoralizing. Such a dog just gives up working and loses confidence in himself and, worse, in his handler. I can remember one test I judged where more than one handler came to the water retrieve and told me that his dog had not retrieved from water before. They still tried the exercise and some, in

doing so, created a problem that would take time to overcome. Do not be afraid to pull your dog out of a test if it proves too difficult. It is better to do that than damage the training and future progress of your dog.

Each exercise in a test should be based on situations that you could encounter on a shooting day. Retrievers will be expected to walk at heel, spaniels to hunt and quarter their ground, and both dogs to retrieve single and multiple seen and unseen dummies, sometimes with distractions on land and water. The complexity of the test depends on the situations created, the type of countryside to be worked and the distances over which the dog has to retrieve. Jumps are often incorporated into an exercise so, if you want to run in tests, train your dog to jump and negotiate obstacles such as walls.

Although tests are more informal than trials, they are run on a similar basis. Arrive on time and let the organizers know that you are on the ground. Pay attention to what is happening. The Test Secretary will call everyone together at the beginning and give you essential information on how the day is to be run. The most important thing to remember is that you are someone else's guest and on his land, and therefore you should respect that land and your host. Do not go wandering around: stay with the competition, and if you do exercise your dog, make sure that it is where you are allowed to do so. Be particularly careful about disturbing livestock, including pheasants. Your association will probably want to use the ground again another year, and you do not want to be the person responsible for their losing it. In the pre-test talk, the Secretary will introduce the judges and any other officials whose instructions or decisions will affect you.

Listen carefully to the judge's instruction.

Unless there is a specific area where you may exercise your dog, keep him on a lead until you come under the judge's control. Continue to keep him on the lead until after the judge has given you instructions and asks you to remove the lead. This will enable you to listen intently to what the judge is telling you, safe in the knowledge that your dog is not wandering away. Make sure that you understand exactly what is required at each exercise; if there is any doubt about what is required or about the location of a hidden dummy, do not be afraid to ask. Some judges will not state the precise location of a hidden dummy but will indicate the area, expecting your dog to use his initiative and nose once he is in this area. If the retrieve is a seen retrieve, both you and your dog will be expected to mark it down. If you do not and the judge has to help you, and you then have to help your dog, you will lose points.

When you remove the lead, put it in your pocket. Trainers have been known to punish their dogs with a lead and so if it is in your hand, tied around your waist or anywhere where your hand can easily grasp it, it could be construed that you are threatening your dog with punishment in order to control him. Do not allow that thought to cross the judge's mind.

At the start of an exercise, check the wind direction and study the lie of the land. Think out the best way of handling the dog to take advantage of scenting conditions and terrain. Have your whistle in your mouth or at least ready for action. In the heat of the moment, many handlers leave their whistles behind in the car or tucked down the front of their jumpers. The jumper problem is a common one and it always causes amusement for the spectators and embarrassment for the handler when there is a rapid fumbling down the front of the jumper when the

133

Wait until the judge tells you to send the dog.

dog is already in action and a command needs to be given.

If you are not the first to run in an exercise, watch how others attempt it and what happens. Keep calm and give yourself time to think – what seems an eternity to you may only be seconds. At the start of your run, compose yourself and your dog and give him clear signals and commands. The moment the lead is off, do not touch your dog, particularly not to line him up for a retrieve or to punish him. I have seen numerous handlers lining their dogs up for an unseen hidden retrieve by kneeling alongside them, manoeuvring their bodies and holding their heads to point them in the right direction. Stand alongside your dog and use your knees and hands to channel and guide him without actually touching him. Wait for the judge to tell you to send your dog:

Clear positive signals and total concentration are required. Whistle ready in hand.

if you send him before being instructed, the judge may think that your dog is unsteady and cannot wait for a required period of time before being sent.

Once your dog is in action, concentrate at all times and do not chat to officials. Concentrate fully until you have completed the whole test and your dog is back on his lead. Many things can and do go wrong when you relax into a false sense of security, thinking that your dog has got a retrieve and it is all over. When asked to send your dog for a retrieve from a specific place, stay at that place. Some competitors will try moving forward, and experienced judges will bring them back with a few choice words. Some of them may even penalize the handler without even giving a warning. If the judge feels that you are struggling on a retrieve, you may be told that you can move forward to

help the dog. If you do (and it is usually a good idea if the judge is advising it), points will be lost. Whatever happens, do not argue with or criticize the judge. Certainly, ask for clarification of an instruction but to show irritation at officials during a test is unsporting and wins no friends.

At most tests, you will be allowed to see the marks you were awarded, and a talk with the judges will help you identify where you went wrong or, better still, what you did well. Accept the judge's opinion and advice, and hold your own counsel. On some matters judges have personal likes and dislikes, and the dog's working style is a particularly individual preference. Judges give their time and experience to help gundog trainers and handlers; it is only right that we treat them with respect. If, for some reason, you do

A water exercise often forms part of a working test.

Judges have their own particular likes and dislikes. This jumping up after delivery may have lost points.

not agree with the judges' decisions, discuss it reasonably with them. You may not agree with their decision, but you may also not fully appreciate all the facts and the basis on which they judged.

The marks that you are given are a measurement of your performance against the standards set by that judge. Some judges will mark hard and penalize you accordingly, others are more lenient. Therefore, it is not always a valuable exercise to compare marks given at different tests under different judges. Assess your own performance critically and, from the comments of the judge and other experienced competitors, determine whether you are improving and what needs to be done in the future to develop you and your dog further.

After the test, competitors will hold a post-mortem and discuss the events of the day. Be honest about your work and if things did not go right, look for reasons why, not excuses or things to blame. The test is to help you, and although it is nice to win or be in the awards, use it as a day to help you and your dog develop and grow together. Should you be lucky enough to win, think about what you did right and build on it for future successes.

With a few exceptions, the prizes at tests are very modest, and certainly will not repay the cost of entering and travelling to the test. The main prize is in the form of a trophy, and the reward is the pride and sense of achievement from the training you have given your dog, and working him well on the day.

12   Field Trials

n any sport, there is always the competi-tive spirit which emerges because of the challenge, the need to be better than someone else and the opportunity to show off your own and, in this case, your dog's abilities. One of the main benefits that comes from competing in field trials is that through the competition, the better working dogs can be seen and selected for future breeding programmes. As field trials are run on game, and take the form of a day's shooting, the performance of the dogs can be watched and assessed as they carry out the job they were really bred for. As the emphasis at a trial is on the dog work and not on the shooting, there is more attention given to the strengths and weaknesses of the dogs, enabling not only judges but also owners, handlers, trainers and spectators to assess their perform-ance.

The winners of trials, and dogs who manage themselves well in these compe-titions, have proved that they can exhibit all the desirable qualities of a good gun-dog and most shooting people selecting a puppy will look through the pedigree for any Field Trial Champions in order to evaluate the type of dog they are consider-ing buying. It must always be remembered that Champions are trained and handled by humans, and some of these are above average trainers. Therefore, before going blindly into obtaining a pup simply because he has a preponderance of FTCH letters in his pedigree, you should try to determine the characteristics of his ancestors and whether those character-istics meet with your requirements. Because a dog is a FTCH, it does not mean that he is more easily trained by the average shooting man. There is no doubt, though, that FTCH in the pedigree attached to either the sire's or dam's name does help breeders to sell puppies, and the advantage for the buyers is that it reduces some of the risk they are taking. With a good working background, a dog who has had success in trials should be free of hard-mouth, giving tongue and gun-shyness.

The qualities of a trials dog are the same as those of a shooting dog, except that his training will have been taken to a higher standard and he should also pos-sess a pace and style that will attract the attention of the judges. I can remember a well-known trialler of spaniels once tell-ing me that a good trials dog should always keep you on your toes. You are always concentrating on him because you think he may step over the mark and make a mistake but, through good train-ing and handling, he rarely does. Running a good trials dog in the field puts many handlers on a high, and after leaving the line and completing a run they often feel drained through intense concentration.

To a great extent, this is where the aims of field trials vary from what actually happens, occasionally to the detriment of the normal handler. A dog who wins a trial may be too much of a dog for the average trainer/handler, and yet we breed from this animal, and his offspring go to shooting homes. In a litter, there will be a number of pups who are fine for the shooting man but, at seven weeks old, it is difficult to tell which ones. The average shooting man has made demands for dogs with field trial parentage, and therefore created a market for this type of dog. A lot of stylish, hard-going, field-trial dogs are easily trained and then handled by the average man, but not all of them. There are no hard and fast rules, other than to think through exactly what you want in a dog and what he is to do for you. Look for one who matches your character and, if field trials are to be your sport, think long and hard. If you are uncertain, ask for advice from disinterested people who know.

Trials dogs and, hence, working dogs, vary a great deal in size and shape. After running once in an Open Spaniel Field Trial, I was told by the judge that the dog I was running was 'too small'. Apart from initially taking great exception to the comment (as this was a dog who had already won a novice stake and taken third in an Open, therefore proving he had ability), it brought to my attention the variety of sizes of gundog today and the shape they are taking.

The features, physique and size of working labradors and spaniels, in particular, vary tremendously and, in both, I have noticed a general move towards the slighter-built dog who looks faster, and attracts attention with his quicker, more exciting action. There is no doubt that in both of these breeds there has been a move away from the standards set down by the Kennel Club, with the exception of a few breeders. I do not think that the move has been a deliberate one, but that it has come about because breeders and trainers have been using dogs in their breeding programmes who have provided the style and hunting ability that

has caught their eye. This fashion in th gundog world has meant that thes smaller dogs have now stamped thei physique into the predominant lines.

I do not think that it is wrong for working Labrador or spaniel to be smalle or even larger than the Kennel Clul standards laid down. I am sure there are number of people who would adamantl state that it is, and that a Labrador shoul look like a Labrador and not a 'Blacl Lurcher', as I have heard them called. Bu even the show fraternity, who say they are breeding to a standard, have stretchec or exaggerated the features.

The working gundog is bred to do a jot – which is to find and retrieve game. Tc this aim, we have sought out and bred from dogs with good noses, gentle mouths, biddable natures, trainability 'handle-ability', and drive in game finding; and most of this searching out has been done through field trials. I certainly like a dog who pleases my eye but, as many who work gundogs know, this does not mean that he has to meet breed standards and, certainly, his working qualities are far more important to me than his beauty. What does have to please my eye, however, is the working action of the dog. Where show people put emphasis on the conformation of the dog, working-dog owners place it on working ability and action.

I have in my own kennel a number of Labradors and Springer Spaniels: not one of them comes anywhere near showing quality. They are, in fact, small- to medium-sized dogs and I like them that way. The small spaniel may not have the weight to drive through thick cover, but I do find that he attacks the cover by finding holes and weaknesses which he uses to get inside and then work game out. The style of the dog can vary according to his

A small Springer Spaniel makes a good retrieve of a cock pheasant in difficult circumstances.

size and, if a particular style becomes popular, breeding from that style of dog will result in a particular size predominating.

By selective breeding, we have developed today's highly responsive and alert gundogs. I would be the first to admit that they are not all perfect, but I am certain that today's top working dogs are every bit as good as and possibly better than those of yesterday whose qualities our memories tend to enhance. Is it just coincidence that they have developed their present stature? Or is it part of the evolutionary process of becoming an improved working dog?

Criticisms levelled at smaller dogs are that they do not have the brain capacity or mouth size to handle game effectively. I have had a number of large-headed dogs through my kennel who have certainly not borne out the brain capacity theory; they may have had large brains but they were not always full of useful thoughts. A dog with a smaller mouth may take a little time to work out how to carry and handle game but, once he has got the knack and balance, he can usually carry it as well as any dog – ask any Cocker Spaniel owner. There may be exceptional cases where a large, strong dog is necessary to do the carrying job well. In wildfowling, a larger, more heavily-built dog will stand up to the rigours of the work far better, and be able to handle geese with less effort. The more traditional-style Labrador also appears to have a more waterproof coat (the double layer of oily fur that sheds water and keeps out the cold). This type of coat is sometimes lacking in the smaller dog.

Large, medium or small, the prime purpose of any working gundog is to do a good job of work. There are some aspects of size that may affect this ability: if such aspects have a detrimental affect on the dog's working ability, they will restrict him and prevent him from working effectively in the field or winning competitions. In both of these cases, responsible owners would not breed from them. As a large proportion of our working dogs originate from field-trial stock that has proven working ability, dogs who are unworkable because of their physique should not appear.

Beauty and style in a dog are in the eye of the beholder. The size of a working dog, within very broad limits, does not bother me. What it must be is a good worker with a character and mental make-up that harmonizes with my own. I have run in trials where there is a prize for the best-looking dog in the awards. In fact, I won one such Labrador trial, but did not feel dismayed when the dog did not win the prize for best looks – in my eyes he was beautiful.

The trials dog, therefore, is not a standard shape or size, but what he must be is a solid working dog, trained to the highest level, with style and pace to set him apart from the other competitors. In spaniels, these two qualities can be the deciding factors which win you the trial. Many spaniel trials are decided at the end by a run off of the two or three top dogs: the one with the best hunting pattern, together with the style and pace that the judges like will be the one that wins. If you are interested in trials and are thinking about buying a dog to run in competitions, spend a considerable amount of time and effort to obtain the right dog for you and competition.

The general standard of dog and handler in today's trials is very high, possibly higher than it has ever been. The amount of interest in gundogs and competition has grown rapidly and to succeed you

need a lot of skill and a good dog along with a certain amount of luck.

Field trials are run on live game, and therefore have to be organized during the shooting season. With some spaniel trials that are run on rabbits this can extend into February, but the standard trialling months are October through to January.

Before entering a trial, it is worth while to attend one or two trials to see what is involved and whether you and your dog are up to the required standard. Although it is run in line with a normal shooting day, the dog work required to pick the shot birds is often more complex. For example, where you might move forward to help your dog to negotiate an obstacle such as a thick hedge or fence on a normal shooting day, at a trial you will be expected to stay at the position from which your dog was sent, and handle from there.

Spaniel trials are often more difficult to watch as a spectator than retriever trials, owing to the nature of the competition: often, they are held in woodland and so the dogs and handlers can be out of sight – all that you know about what is happening comes from handlers who have run and are returning to the waiting group, or from what you can surmise from the sounds in the wood. If you volunteer to help by carrying game or stewarding (for which you will need a little training yourself), you are going to be among the dogs and will see the action. Some trials are held in open ground or on hillsides where the view is better. Triallers who have run on the ground before and who know the area will be able to advise you about how easy it is to watch.

Many clubs that run trials welcome helpers. By being involved, watching and listening, you can get a better idea of what is happening and why. The Kennel Club lays down rules and guide-lines for the conduct of a trial and the judging of the dogs, and to read these is also a must. After gaining some experience and knowledge, you can decide whether trialling is for you and your dog. Whatever you do, however, do not enter a dog who is not adequately trained or has had insufficient experience. It has been known for some competitors to enter dogs who have not even handled freshly shot game. If your dog has performed well at tests, has a gentle mouth, is quiet, has handled freshly shot game, including runners, and works with good style and pace, then it is worth a try – but first you have to get a run.

Although you do not have to belong to a gundog club to get a run, it is more expensive to enter if you are not a member, and members take preference over non-members in the draw. Today's trials are very over-subscribed – retriever trials in particular – and it is not unknown for eighty to one hundred members to apply for a run in a stake that may be limited to twelve dogs.

There are gundog clubs throughout the country and, apart from the few exceptions who limit their membership in some way, you can become a member of all of them. The limiting factor is the distance you are willing to travel to run in a trial. The Kennel Club has a list of all affiliated gundog clubs who run trials, together with their Secretaries' names and addresses. The Kennel Gazette each year lists the trials that are run by those clubs. Joining a club is straightforward: write a letter or make a telephone call to the Secretary asking for an application form; fill this in and send it off with the appropriate joining fee and subscription – usually a nominal amount. The application form will often require a proposer and seconder. If you are new to gundog competition you may not know anyone in the club, but a good Secretary will generally get over this difficulty for you either by getting a proposer or seconder for you or inviting you to a club event where you can meet other members. This formality should not create any barriers for you.

There are no set patterns to the way that clubs are run. Some exist purely for field trials, others have social events and training classes as well as tests and trials. Clubs such as the United Retriever Club are nation-wide and have regional operations, although their trials are run on a national basis.

The Kennel Club defines a field trial as 'a meeting for the purpose of holding competitions to assess the work of gundogs in the field, with dogs working on live unhandled game where game may be shot'. There is an emphasis on unhandled game, as any game that has been handled must not be used to test the dogs in any part of a field trial. The only exception is if a water test is carried out to determine whether the dogs will enter water freely or in a test for the award of the Show Gundog Working Certificate.

To run a recognized field trial, the club must be registered with the Kennel Club and be given the authority to organize field trials. They must also have obtained a licence for each field trial they run. Unless this is all correct, you cannot gain the recognized titles for your dog from competition. Many newcomers to the sport also confuse tests with trials, and in doing so are either misled or mislead others on the ability and status of certain dogs.

Once you are a member of a recognized gundog club you will receive the schedules for the field trials, which detail all the

Dogs waiting for the water test at a Spaniel Championship.

A water test in progress at a Spaniel Championship with two judges in very close attendance.

particulars of the trial. These schedules contain important and relevant information, which includes the following:

(a) the date and venue of the field trial;
(b) the time and place of meeting prior to the start of the trial;
(c) the definition of each stake to be held and number of runners in each stake – the definition being Open, All-Aged, Novice or Puppy;
(d) the details of entry fees and prizes;
(e) the latest date – and usually which post – for receipt of entry applications;
(f) the date, place and time of the draw, and the method of notifying results;
(g) a statement that the field trial is to be held under Kennel Club Field Trial Regulations;
(h) Notice of any restrictions or conditions attached to the stakes, including arrangements for substitution of dogs;
(i) the names of the judges, if known;
(j) if more than one stake, the order in which the stakes will be run;

With the schedule, you will also receive an entry form where you enter details about yourself, and the dog you are entering. Once this has been filled in and received by the club, that is the dog you will be required to run, unless the club allows substitution for specific reasons.

Entries received by the closing date are graded in order of preference (if there is one). For example, members of a club will be drawn before non-members; if the stake is an Open Stake, dogs who have qualified for Open Stakes will take preference over dogs who have not.

Some societies add their own requirements, which you must also observe. Generally, these include sending a stamped addressed envelope with your application and the correct entry fee.

Failure to do either of these can result in your application not being put in the draw. Once you have sent off your entry, obtaining a run in a field trial then needs a certain amount of luck, because there will be a draw. The applications are graded as required, placed in the hat, and the order in which they are drawn determines the running order of the trial.

A few days after the draw you will receive notification of the running order. If luck is on your side, you will be among those who have got a definite run; if not, you will be in the reserves. There does not appear to be any pattern to the way in which dogs drop out of a stake prior to the day of running, but do not despair if you are way down on the list of reserves. I have been rung up by the Field Trial Secretary and offered a run when I have been so far down the list of reserves that there seemed to be no hope. Dogs and handlers pull out for various reasons, such as a bitch coming into season; and the organizer then has to burn up telephone time trying to find someone to fill that vacant space. Some handlers may be running dogs elsewhere, or it may be too late in the day to arrange time off work or reorganize plans. If you can be the 'available one' you will be surprised how often you will be able to get a run.

There are four types of stake that you can enter with your dog. An Open Stake is one in which the dogs have the opportunity of gaining a qualification (whole or part) for the title of Field Trial Champion. By obtaining qualifications, dogs can also gain entry to the Championships or Champion Stake for their breed. An Open Stake is open to all dogs of a specified breed or breeds. Generally, an Open Stake is limited to a prescribed number of runners. These runners will be decided upon by a draw, as previously described, and preference will be given according to previous performance.

An All-Aged Stake is one that is open to all dogs of a specified breed or breeds, without restriction as to their age. However, restrictions may be placed upon the stake by the organising society. Awards in these stakes do not represent qualifications towards the title of Field Trial Champion.

A Novice Stake is for dogs who have not gained a first, second or third in Open Stakes or first or one second (retriever breeds) in other stakes. This stake is the first step in the ladder of competition and, in the main, dogs have to take first or one second (for retriever breeds) before they progress to the Open Stakes.

A Puppy Stake is confined to dogs under 2 years old on the date of the field trial. These stakes are not common and are not an essential part of the trial structure. They do, however, give young dogs early experience of trials, and provide handlers with an idea of how their dog is performing in competition.

Retriever trials may be one- or two-day trials. A one-day trial will usually have 12 dogs. In stakes other than Open, up to 16 dogs are sometimes run, depending on whether the club feels they can give each dog enough work and retrieves to judge them fairly. Three or four judges will officiate at a trial; a one-day trial usually has three judges officiating; and a two-day trial has 24 runners and, as a rule, four judges. For spaniel trials, which, with the exception of the Championship, are one-day events, there are 16 runners and two judges.

The judges at trials are responsible for the actual judging, for ensuring that the trial is conducted under Kennel Club Regulations, and for the schedule for the stake. Judges of trials are experienced dog trainers, handlers and competitors who have been asked by clubs to officiate at the trials. The Kennel Club controls and maintains a list of top level judges (the 'A' panel) and a second level (the 'B' panel). All trials must have at least one 'A' panel judge as part of the judging team.

The main job of the judges at any trial is to find the dog who pleases them most with the quality of his work to the gun in the shooting field, on that particular day. The last point is an important one, and judges have to ignore any occurrences that they have witnessed on days or in stakes other than the one they are currently judging. When talking to judges or competitors, the statement, 'It was the best dog on the day' is often heard. Dogs, like people, have off days and it would be wrong to have judging influenced by what has happened at other times, but sufficient work should be given to a dog during the main body of a stake to test his full capabilities and expose any weaknesses. The most important aspect of the work that a judge should be looking for is natural game-finding ability.

Judges will try their best to give all dogs the opportunity of working well, but not every dog has the same opportunities, and each dog has a unique run, simply because a trial is run as close to a normal shooting day as possible. It is often said that good handlers make their own luck, but there is no doubt that luck does play a part in a trial. A bird that is wounded and runs creates problems and, if not found, can lose you marks if your dog was the first to try for it. However, you can turn this situation to your advantage: if your dog finds and retrieves that bird, the judge will credit you highly for finding a difficult bird.

A judge will mark your dog's performance by grading it 'A', 'B' or 'C' with the addition of a plus or minus, if required. In addition, extra notes will be made on the work you and your dog have done, and will be taken into account by the judges.

Retrievers and spaniels will be required to retrieve shot game on command. Wounded game will take priority over dead game and the judge will usually ask you to pick this first where practical. The judge will instruct you when and from where to send your dog for a retrieve. If you have not seen where the game has fallen, the judge may give you instructions, but do not expect them to be precise to the exact square yard. It is not always easy to mark each bird that falls; although at retriever trials, many societies have markers, who note where each bird comes down. Your dog may have marked the fall even if you have not, but, even if the judge gives you a general area, it is the task of your dog, as a game-finder, to do the rest. I can remember very well one lesson I was taught at a retriever trial, by a very eminent judge. The drive had been completed and the judge told me to send my dog for a bird that had fallen into some scrub below where we stood. I asked where the bird was, and was asked by the judge why I had not marked it down. Upon replying that I was watching my dog (to make sure he did not move), he politely told me that at this standard of competition my dog should be trustworthy and I should be helping him by marking and remembering where birds have fallen. He was right, of course.

In some cases, game is shot too close to a dog (particularly in retriever trials) to be of any value as a retrieve. This retrieve may be offered to a dog under another judge who may or may not accept it for the dog running under him. In a spaniel trial, the dog will generally be given the opportunity of retrieving the game that he has flushed and that has been shot. If that dog has already had a retrieve, and retrieves are in short supply, other retrieves may be offered to dogs who have not had one so that their retrieving ability and mouth can be tested.

In a retriever trial, dogs will be required, during the first round, to retrieve game shot by their own Guns, unless the retrieve is of no value where it fell. These retrieves may be offered to other dogs or, in some cases, the judges may move the dog a distance away from the retrieve before asking for its collection. In the second round of a retriever trial, it will not matter which Gun shot the game because this will not determine which dog is sent. In the event of a dog failing to find a retrieve, more dogs may be called in to attempt it. If a subsequent dog finds the retrieve, the previous dogs will be discarded as this becomes an 'eye wipe'.

Where game is wounded and is running, the Judges will mark the performance of the dog and his attempts to find the runner. If the dog is not making a very good job of going to the fall and taking a line on the runner, he will be called up quickly and another dog put on to it. These subsequent dogs may be taken closer to the fall of the game as they may not have had the opportunity of marking the fall. The order in which they are run will be taken into account when their work is judged: the first dog has the advantage of seeing the fall and working on a fresh line in fresh ground; later dogs tried will have to contend with ground fouled by earlier dogs and a more stale line. If the runner is found by a subsequent dog it is again an eye wipe. If no game is found and the first dog had made a good attempt at locating it by going directly to the fall and taking a line on the

A good clear signal using body, leg and arms. Whistle ready for action.
A single judge watches closely.

runner, he should not be discarded and can still feature in the awards.

In all trials, good marking by a dog in all types of crop and cover is essential. This will enable the dog to make a straight run to the fall of the game, which will cause minimum disturbance of un-shot game. In the shooting field, you do not want a dog who runs over a wide area flushing game and therefore denying you a future shot. A dog who goes directly to the fall and then shows good game-finding ability will get a high grade. Even when a dog has not marked the fall and is given a direction on the cast off, he should bring his game-finding ability into play and require the minimum of handling. Where hand signals are used, the dog should obey them promptly. These dogs make retrieving look easy and their hand-lers appear to have little to do – most of the handler's work has, of course, gone into the dog's earlier training to produce this effect.

The pick up of the game should be clean and quick, followed by a speedy and direct return to the handler. Inexperi-enced dogs and ones with very gentle mouths can have difficulty carrying some game. Young pheasants at the beginning of the season can create this type of problem, and the dog will only be penal-ized if he plays about with the retrieve, mouths it or puts it down for a period of time. The dog who rests the game on the ground but does not release it, only re-adjusting his grip so that he can get it safely back to his handler, should not be over penalized. If your dog puts the game down in order to shake after a water retrieve, this can be heavily penalized. So, it is important that when your dog leaves the water, he comes at a fast pace up to you and delivers the retrieve before shaking.

The moment game is delivered to you by your dog, it should be handed to the judge who will examine it immediately for signs of hard-mouth. This is where the dog has physically damaged the bird by crushing in one or both sides of the ribs. This is a serious fault and dogs who are found to do this are disqualified. To check for hard-mouth, the judge will place the game on the palm of the hand, breast upward, head away from the Judge's body and then, using thumb and fore-fingers, feel for caved in, flat or broken ribs. A small amount of pressure from the free hand on the breast bone of the game will often assist in feeling for any damage. If there is any suspicion of hard-mouth, the game should be passed to the co-judges for their examination and agreement. As it is a serious fault which can not only cause a dog to be disqualified but also ruin his reputation, judges are very careful to make correct decisions and to study all the details of the shooting. If there is any doubt, the dog will be given the benefit of it, but you can expect future game he retrieves in the trial to be very thoroughly examined.

If your dog is suspected of hard-mouth you will also be given the opportunity of examining the game with the judges. In these circumstances, it is worth remembering that the judge's decision is final and arguing does you little good. If your retrieve was a runner, particularly if it was a bird, the judge will look for this to be returned with its head up and very lively looking. If, on the way back, the head falls and the bird dies, a very close inspection for damage can be expected. With runners, there is often the possibility of skin damage when the dog catches them from behind, and many strong, running pheasants return with tail feathers missing and rumps gashed as a result of a struggle, or of inexperience on the part of the dog. Early on in the season, some

birds will die apparently through shock, and actual damage will not have been the cause. Experienced judges know of this possibility and, providing the bird shows no evidence of damage, will discount it.

Should you be unfortunate enough to be disqualified for hard-mouth, make a point of checking the future game retrieved by this dog. The damage may not have been caused by the dog biting the game. On occasions, your dog will have to negotiate thick hedges and fences, or struggle up steep banks, which can push the bird on to the teeth of the dog and cause damage. The judges can only judge what they see and if they do not see an obvious cause, other than the dog's mouth, they can occasionally reach the wrong conclusion. So do not condemn your dog out of hand: investigate the possibility of hard-mouth by examining future game.

When working your dog in a trial, whether retriever or spaniel, there are certain important points that you must remember as, if overlooked, these can reflect badly on your grading or even have you put out of the trial. The moment you are called to the line and are under the judge, you will be expected to listen and take instructions. When asked to remove your lead, do so immediately and put it away in your pocket. The lead should be out of sight where it does not pose a threat to the dog. This is also true of a stick: the carrying of a stick is not allowed, except in cases where the handler needs it because of a disability.

Once your dog has come under the judge, you should refrain from touching him: the dog must be seen to be under control without resorting to physical contact. At one trial, where I was judging with a very experienced 'A' panel Judge, the dog he was watching was becoming a bit of a handful. The handler realized this and called his dog up to him with a stern voice and reached down as though to administer an ear tug. Very quickly the judge stopped this action by saying 'Touch him and I will put you out!'. The dog was not touched but a few minutes later he was out of control and out of the trial. If your dog cannot be controlled in a trial without physical correction, he should not be running. A trial is not the place to correct your dog physically: if he does wrong, you will be very poorly thought of if you rush out and shake or hit him – you will be out of the trial and you may also be reported to the society running the trial, and even to the Kennel Club, for misconduct. I have heard some

triallers say that their dog only does one particular thing wrong when at a trial and therefore they cannot correct it any other way. If this is the case, do not trial him, or work hard at making your dog think he is at a trial by simulating the situation and then correcting him. A trial is not a training ground.

Listen to the Judges' instructions and make sure you understand exactly what is required. Ask, if you do not know, but do so in a polite way. There are times when you may disagree with what the judge requires. A good example is when you are asked to retrieve a bird and are given a mark of the fall which you think is wrong. This can be a difficult situation: do you say that you think the judge is wrong, or do you send your dog who might not find a bird? Remember that you might be wrong and a bird could have fallen when you were concentrating elsewhere. If in doubt, ask politely for clarification and then make a full effort to do what the judge instructs. If, as in this example, there was no bird, the judge will take into account your efforts to carry out the retrieve and would not penalize you, giving you another chance of a retrieve later.

The quieter you can be in handling the dog the better. Too much whistling and particularly too much shouting will certainly reflect badly in your grading. Nerves can play a dramatic role in the way you conduct yourself at a trial, and it is surprising how much more you whistle and panic at a trial than you would when working your dog under normal circumstances.

From the moment you enter the line under the judge to the moment you return to the waiting competitors, do not lose concentration and relax, unless it is controlled relaxation. Your dog may

The judge will clearly explain what he requires. If in doubt, ask.

An excellent find and retrieve but don't relax until it is in your hand.

have made an excellent find of a bird and is returning to you; you lose concentration and may even turn to say a word to the judge or fellow competitor. In the past, many faults have occurred in that moment and, doubtless, will continue to do so in the future. Your dog, realizing that you have lost concentration, may put the bird down and go off hunting elsewhere; he may change birds or lose direction and look very novice-like as he searches for you among the sea of faces in the line. There are many things that can go wrong when you lapse into a false sense of security, so keep up the concentration. Once your dog has delivered the retrieve, make him sit and wait until you are given another instruction. Some spaniels are prone to go off hunting again, which looks

extremely sloppy; and some retrievers bounce about and jump up at their handlers, which not only looks bad but, practically, could be dangerous if the dog was retrieving to a Gun. In jumping up, the dog could collide with the shotgun and cause a misfire.

RETRIEVER TRIALS

There are two ways in which a retriever trial is run. One is a driven shoot where the dogs are sat among the Guns and birds are driven over them and shot as on a normal shooting day. The second method is a walk-up. A walk-up is where the dogs actually in the competition at that time are walked in a line which contains

149

Dog too far ahead

Figs 16–18   Walking to heel.

Dog too far behind

Fig 17

Best position for control

Fig 18

them plus judges, Guns, stewards and occasionally some additional beaters. A walk-up is often done in root crops such as sugar-beet and stubble turnip. Although common in trials – and some trials attempt to include both driven shooting and a walk-up – I have rarely walked up game in this way with a retriever on a proper shooting day. I am therefore uncertain why many clubs make a concerted effort to include a walk-up but this is certainly one aspect of trial work you and your dog must contend with. Experience of working in root crops is therefore essential.

If you go to trials in the eastern counties, this root crop is likely to be sugar-beet, which can and often does create many problems for a dog. Whether this is caused by the rustling of the crisp leaves, the way scent is held under the canopy of the foliage or other factors I cannot say, but working a dog in sugar-beet is an experience in itself. Dogs who are normally prompt on the whistle and under control in other types of cover can become difficult to handle and hold. Walking in roots, the dog must be able to contend with birds running around often under the feet, and flushing in front of them. The field may be 'hot' with live game, which the dog has to ignore. When a bird is flushed and shot, the dog is sent immediately for the retrieve and therefore may run through live, unshot game which will flush around him. Your dog must be steady to this and be able to recognize the scent of a shot bird, ignoring all other temptations. A dog who has marked the fall and has that retrieve fixed in his mind,

ignoring all other distractions, is more likely to succeed. He should be able to take long, straight lines through the crop, even though he may be running against the crop rows. He must be on the whistle, stopping promptly and taking directions accurately in this difficult and demanding form of trialling.

On a driven shoot trial, the dogs who are sat in the line with the Guns will not be required to retrieve until the end of the drive. Where you sit your dog is your decision. Some handlers sit their dogs in front, facing them. The dog can then look past the handler and mark birds falling behind the line. It also reduces some of the temptation to run in as the dog would have to pass the handler. Other handlers

At a retriever trial, the beginning of a walk up in roots.

Handling a dog in roots can be difficult. Notice the closeness of the judge, the Gun and other competitors, making it difficult for your dog to pick you out when he looks back.

A driven shoot in progress, with dogs sat in front of handlers.

A good clear direction with the dog watching the handler's hand.
The judge will often mark where you have to send the dog from, in
this case the stick.

A busy driven-shoot line-up. Guns, judges, stewards and markers take the line as well as dogs and handlers. Handlers show different preferences for where to sit their dogs.

sit them alongside themselves, which is a natural position and one in which, if the dog is sat at a slight angle, he can see in front and behind.

At a drive where a lot of birds are falling around the dogs, the temptations will be great. In an Open Trial, the birds falling near a dog are often left there until the end of the drive, but at a Novice Trial these birds are likely to be picked up by the judge, particularly if they are flapping. In the shooting field, a dog is expected to deal mainly with runners and birds that are not easily found because they have fallen in heavy cover. At a driven trial, because there is a time delay between when the bird is shot and when the dog is sent, few real runners are picked. An official picker-up is on call to deal with these birds, as required, once the trial retrieving has been completed. Retrievers are rarely required to work heavy cover such as brambles and gorse in a trial and, if cover is thick, it has been known to

cause a few dogs and their handlers considerable difficulty. Any good gundog should be able to handle a variety of cover and so, to avoid any embarrassment, make sure that you have trained your dog to deal with it.

In the body of a field-trial stake, a retriever is required to be steady by the handler, whether walking up and flushing the game or sitting at a drive. The dog should also be steady when the shots are fired over him: he should not move until his handler commands him to seek for wounded or dead game and retrieve it. Retrieves can be expected to be on land and water. Where three judges officiate, they judge individually, but where a four-judge system is employed, they judge in pairs. Unless a dog is eliminated from the stake, he must be tried and run under more than one judge. The Chief Steward will attempt to send the dogs into the line in numerical order. After the first run, this can be difficult – some dogs being kept

Retrieves are not always straightforward. This Golden Retriever is being sent through a narrow gate into a release pen for a retrieve.

longer in the line owing to the time taken for retrieves under their judge – and consequently they may be sent to the judges in any order.

Dogs brought into the line under the judges are placed so that the lowest number is on the right. In the three-judge system, each judge will have two dogs. The first bird selected by the judge to be retrieved is given to the right-hand dog, the next bird to the left-hand dog. When the first dog has been given two retrieves in the first round, he will be taken up from the line and the left-hand dog moved to the right of the judge; a new replacement dog is brought in by the Steward and sat on the left.

If a dog fails on a retrieve, i.e. he cannot find it, his running companion will be tried. If this dog succeeds and 'wipes the eye' of the dog who failed, the failed dog is discarded from the line and the next bird is automatically for the dog who succeeded (if this success was on his first retrieve). If he succeeded on his second retrieve, he will be taken up to await the second round. An eye wipe will usually up-grade the dog who completed it and, as the handler, you can feel pleased that you have done a noteworthy retrieve, even though you may also feel a little upset at having put out another trialler. If both dogs fail on a retrieve, other dogs may be brought in to attempt it. Up to four further dogs may be tried: if they fail, the judges will walk out and look for the bird. If the bird is found by the judges, all dogs who have tried will be marked down – the first dog to attempt the retrieve particularly so. If the bird is not found, only the first dog down is penalized.

Providing they have not committed any eliminating faults, all dogs should be given a run under a second judge. In a four-judge system, they will already have run under two judges working as a pair – therefore, some dogs may not be called into the second round. Whatever system is employed, handlers may not wish to take a second-round run based on their

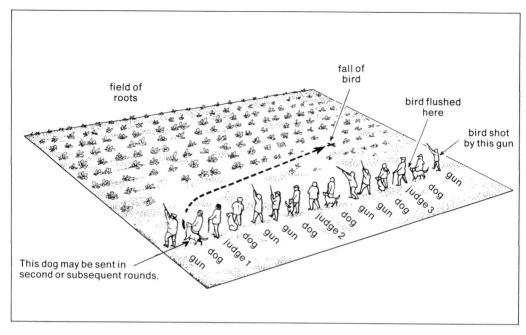

Fig 19 Retriever trial. Second round, down-the-line retrieves, retrieving
in front or behind the line. (Walk up.)

earlier performance. In the second round, each dog is given one retrieve, but the proceedings are often changed to increase the complexity of the retrieves.

The amount of time given to a dog to complete a retrieve depends upon the situation and whether the judge feels that the dog is making a workman-like job of it. If the dog is taking a lot of handling and is not getting to the fall area, possibly even disturbing unshot game, a judge is within his rights to call that dog up. Some birds may fall into a location that creates difficulties for the dogs and so, in the judge's opinion, is not a fair retrieve – these birds will be scratched (not counted) and any work done by the dogs discounted. A dog who makes a retrieve look easy because he has marked well or handles easily should be given good grades. It does often happen that a retrieve is made to look difficult by the actions of a dog and handler, but experienced judges will be able to determine the complexity

of a retrieve and grade accordingly.

After completion of the second run, the judges will compare their assessments of the dogs and the notes they have made on their performance. The top dogs, who have the same gradings, will be brought forward for the run off. In this, all dogs and handlers are brought close together and the judges work together as a team to make the final decision. Being close together, the temptation created by other dogs passing as they go out for retrieves and return is much greater. It is also more difficult for dogs to mark falling game when they are bunched together and, in this situation, good handling becomes essential. The judges are able to assess the partnership of dog and handler. Although it is a pleasure to watch a dog who goes with pace and style, in retriever trials this is not as important as it is in spaniel trials. The judges may like the appearance of a dog and the way he works, but unless he completes the retrieves and

Judges put their heads together and compare notes.

has the luck to obtain some of the important trial-winning ones, such as runners or eye wipes, he will not come to the top.

The Kennel Club regulations state that a dog will be eliminated from the stake if he is found to have hard-mouth, he whines or barks, runs in or chases game, is out of control, fails to enter water on command or changes game while retrieving (picks one head of game and, instead of returning promptly to the handler, puts it down to pick other game). Other major faults are failing to find dead or wounded game, unsteadiness at heel, having his eye wiped, disturbing ground that has not been previously shot, slack and unbusiness-like work, noisy handling and poor control. In certain circumstances, these major faults become eliminating faults. For instance, it is usual for a dog who has been eye wiped to be eliminated or a dog who is disturbing ground and is not quickly brought back to a fall area and under control by his handler to be called up by the judge and eliminated. This is particularly the case when a dog has moved on to the second round or is in the final stages of the trial. The reason for this is that the dogs left in the stake by this stage will be expected to be of a higher standard and so, unless there are extenuating circumstances, the judges will not be as lenient as they may have been in the initial stages.

Judging is not an easy job and one always tries to be fair in giving every dog a chance of success. At the end of the day, however, the dogs have to be sorted out and graded, in order to come to a decision. Positive judging will do this by providing opportunities for the dogs to do well and by understanding the situations that arise, which will give the handlers and dogs every opportunity to work well. Some judging can be negative, where the emphasis is on finding ways to eliminate dogs, sometimes quite harshly, until the remaining dogs can be graded into the winning order.

Once the run off has been completed (if one is required), the Chief Steward will declare the trial finished and everyone then returns to the meeting point for the awards. If you are the one lucky enough to win, be prepared to give a vote of thanks to the judges, which is not too difficult if they put you first.

SPANIEL TRIALS

A spaniel comes into his own when game is not too plentiful and cover is such that the dog needs to hunt and push out all possible game-holding places to provide the Gun with a shot. Ideally, spaniel grounds are woodland, rough bramble and bracken-covered ground, reeds and long, white grass where game is available for the dog who is prepared to work to find it. Occasionally, root crops such as fodder beet, turnip and sugar-beet will need to be worked. These are often part of intensive game-holding covers and produce, if anything, too much game at once. However, you must be prepared for work in such crops and give your dog experience of handling what can be difficult cover. Sugar-beet is very demanding cover to work and tests your control over the dog to the full.

My first experience of this crop was at a trial in Essex, where I was running way down the list. Watching the first few dogs, I was quite amazed at how difficult they were to control and falsely thought that their handlers had brought them into trials without having given them the necessary amount of training and experience. Neither my dog nor I had any experience of sugar-beet – other root crops

At a spaniel trial, dog and handler hunting cover under the eye of the judge.

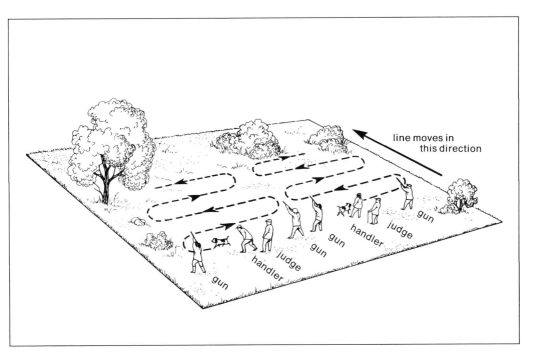

line moves in
this direction

gun

judge

handler

gun

gun

handler

judge

gun

Fig 20   Trial line at a spaniel trial.

we had worked but not this one. However, I did not see any difference between
working the dog in turnip or sugar-beet,
so went into the line confidently. The
moment I cast my dog off to hunt, I
realized that things were very different.
The dog had stepped up a gear and was
hunting with an added zest, which meant
that I had to work hard, and concentrate
to the full, to hold him, and this, in my
own opinion, required far too much
whistle. After completing each of my
runs, I felt totally drained. We took a
commendable second that day, but I
certainly did not underestimate the
attraction of sugar-beet again.

In a spaniel trial, dogs are run, where
possible, in pairs. Two judges officiate
and one dog will run under each judge.
There are two main runs: for the first, the
odd numbers will run under the right-
hand judge (who is usually the senior
judge) and, unless they are eliminated,
will then wait until called to the left-hand

judge for the second run. The even-
numbered dogs are run under the left-
hand judge first, and then wait to be
called to the right-hand judge for their
second run.

Each judge has two Guns who will
walk either side of the handler. The
judges will usually place the Guns about
15 to 20 yards away. This does vary, and
Guns do not always maintain their set
position. Owing to the lie of the countryside, and the manner in which the dog is
being hunted, the Guns may bunch up
with the dog or move further away. This
can cause problems as your brief is to
work the ground between the Guns. The
Guns should not, however, walk ahead of
the dog as this can disturb game before
the dog has reached the area. Most
experienced judges will be able to advise
and explain what is required to the Guns
who do not know the procedure, but if
Guns do go wrong, remember it is probably they who have given you the day,

159

and tact and politeness are the correct approach, through the judge.

A spaniel is a hunting dog and will be expected, at all times, to work ground within range of the shotgun, find game and flush it. The ground treatment should take into account the terrain and wind direction, but should ensure that no game is missed on the beat he is running. The speed of the line will be dictated by the judges who will ensure that the dog gets every opportunity of making good all the ground he is asked to hunt. The eliminating faults for a spaniel are the same as for a retriever, except that a spaniel can also be eliminated for missing game on the beat. If game is missed and is flushed behind the line on ground that has already been walked over, the judges will take into account the speed of the line and the type of cover being hunted. In some cover, particularly root crops, birds tend to run rather than fly, and can quite easily dodge through the line and take off behind the dog. In addition to the eliminating faults, a spaniel will be penalized severely if he does not quarter his ground effectively, does not stop to shot and flush, or catches unwounded game (pegs).

A judge will try to give you the opportunity of completing all aspects of spaniel work: the hunt, the flush, the sit to shot and the retrieve. However, if for any reason you do no complete any of these in the first run, tell the second judge this when you are called in line under him. Unless you have completed all the stages of spaniel work successfully, you should not feature in the awards. Again, this is where luck plays an essential role.

At the start of your run, the Judge will tell you the direction of the beat and often point out a landmark to head for. On open ground, such as long grass and reeds, you should keep a straight line with your dog working between the Guns. In more dense cover, it is advisable to move with the dog to keep him in sight. Where there are high clumps of cover such as laurels, rhododendrons or gorse you should help the dog by moving from clump to clump, directing him to hunt each one through. Where this has been the type of cover encountered at a trial, most judges I have run under have told me to work any cover on the beat that is likely to hold game and to move about. I do know that some judges may not like too much moving about but this certainly would be the procedure on a normal shooting day. If you have any doubt about the attitude of the judge, ask if you can move to the cover with your dog. An Open Trial spaniel should not need as much guidance from you as a novice and, again, judges will be looking for the right standard of hunting, training and experience.

A spaniel is expected to have drive and face cover well, he should be exciting and pleasing to watch and be responsive to his handler's commands. The spaniel who does his work with little help from his handler, and who has style, pace and drive, is the one who will rise to the top. This dog should show himself during one of his runs to be a good game-finder and one blank run should not eliminate him from the placings. To be among the top placings, however, a dog must have shown that he can complete all aspects of his work and will, therefore, have hunted, flushed and retrieved game.

Although pegging of game is a major fault and dogs are eliminated for this, judges will take into consideration the situation in which it occurred. Birds trapped within bramble thickets, unable to escape, are easily caught by a dog, and myxomatosis rabbits are readily picked.

If the dog has made a concerted effort to grab and catch the game, this should be marked down.

Where the pegging was unavoidable (the game could not get away), if the handler can make the dog release the game with a verbal command and it escapes unscathed, the dog will not be penalized. If he will not release the game or, after release, it cannot fly or run, it will be checked for damage. Some game may have been shot on earlier shoots and so is unable to evade capture. They will also be giving off a wounded scent, which encourages the dog to pick them. Judges will check very thoroughly any pegged game that comes to hand, looking for damage from shot. Broken tail feathers, wing tips, blood on the beak, shot lying under the skin are all signs of gunshot wound. Such wounds mut be taken into account and the dog allowed to continue unpenalized.

If the bird has been damaged by the dog, the dog will be eliminated. Many pegged birds are damaged by the dog as he extricates it from cover or even from a rabbit-hole that stopped the bird escaping. Even if the bird is not damaged in any way, some judges will still eliminate a dog for pegging. However, I have attended trials where, at the beginning of the trial, the judges have announced that no dog will be eliminated for pegging unless the game is damaged by the dog.

Upon flushing game or a shot being fired, the spaniel should stop. If the 'Stop' whistle is blown as a reaction to the flush, or just to remind the dog what is required, this is acceptable. If the 'Stop' whistle is blown because the dog was about to chase, most judges would mark this down. Experienced judges will notice the difference. Sitting or dropping to flush or shot is an added refinement and will probably catch the judge's eye. If the dog is in thick cover, he may move to the edge of the cover to mark the fall. This is considered to show intelligence, but he must stop immediately he has moved into the open.

Some spaniels will point or hesitate before flushing game; this may be inherited or it may have been taught to the dog by the handler. Provided the dog will flush on command, this is also considered to be a refinement in the Kennel Club Regulations. Some judges, however, prefer a strong, flushing dog who does not hesitate so, if your dog does have a tendency to do this, do not let him hesitate long. False hesitation or pointing will be particularly disliked by most judges. Ground-game is deemed to have flushed the moment it moves or leaves cover. A bird flushes the moment it leaves the ground and flies. A bird that runs can cause a problem as the dog should push it until it flies. But how far should the dog be allowed to push? You must decide that at the time, depending on the circumstances. If the bird is pushed too far, it will not give the Gun a shot, but if the dog is called off too early, he will not have made the flush, which he should have done.

This dilemma happened to me in a trial in Sussex: my dog had worked hard on a hen pheasant that had tucked in and then decided to run along tracks in long white grass. The hen was in full view with the dog inches behind its tail. 'Fly', I silently shouted in my mind. About 15 yards later, it must have heard my pleas and took off. Unfortunately, my dog was so intent on the bird that my training flew off with the bird, and even the 'Stop' whistle was ignored for far too many steps. Out of the trial we went, with another example of the luck that is needed in the game. Had that bird flushed promptly, I am confident that the dog would have stopped immediately as usual.

Spaniel hunting should have pace and style, coupled with game-finding ability. Pace is not raw speed. Some spaniels are fast but run their pattern disturbing game rather than finding it and flushing. Speed has to be matched by the nose and intelligent use of scent. Cover should be investigated, in fact, attacked to make any game inside aware that the only way to go is out. A good spaniel is a mover of game. With experience and natural gunsense, a spaniel will learn to bring the game out towards the Gun where he knows there is more likelihood of it being shot with a resulting retrieve. The scenting conditions will tend to make a spaniel adjust his pace and hunting accordingly, but a spaniel who potters or just does not go with any enthusiasm should be discarded. A good handler knows when this is happening and will often pull the dog out of the stake. Whatever the reason for the dog not working well, it is not worth causing any further problems for the handler or the dog. False pointing or falsely indicating game is irritating, and after crying wolf a few times a Gun loses his trust in the dog. The result is that interest in the work is lost and if a bird is flushed, the Gun may not be prepared. False pointing is, again, heavily penalized.

Passing or missing game is a major fault where the dog has moved on past game which is later flushed. As a handler, you can help the dog by ensuring that he does cover all the ground on his beat and does not miss even the smallest amount of cover. It is surprising how even the smallest tussock of grass or low pile of sticks can hide game that may not be giving off much scent. Keep your eyes open as you hunt your dog and concentrate on getting him within scenting range of any game-holding cover. Do not walk too fast: if you move forward for a retrieve, make sure that you come back to the original spot and hunt the cover around it as you move off; and just because you have flushed game from one piece of cover, do not expect that there will not be more game in there. With some cover, it is difficult to determine whether the dog did actually miss game or whether the game ran around the dog and behind the line. This can happen in cover such as root crops and bracken, where the canopy hides the birds and they tend to run under this foliage rather than fly. If a judge is of the opinion that you have missed game, he should tell you immediately. He may not put you out but it will be marked against you.

As the main job of the spaniel is to find game through hunting, the quality of the retrieve is not as important as it is in retriever trials. However, the dog should pick up cleanly, return promptly at a good speed and deliver well up to hand. If the dog has had a long, hard hunt, the judges will take this into account when watching the retrieve. Your dog will be asked to retrieve the game he has flushed, and which has been shot, unless he has already had a retrieve and the judges are looking for a retrieve for his opposite number that is running. Where a spaniel has already completed a retrieve that has tested his mouth and retrieving skills, the judges may offer retrieves to each other or bring in a dog who has previously completed a run but did not get a retrieve, so allowing him to complete one of the important tasks of spaniel work.

If your dog marks the bird that has been shot, the judge will ask you to send him from the position where he stopped.

When the bird is a runner, falls a long distance away, or disappears behind an obstruction, you may be told to move forward, but do not do so unless instructed by the judge. Where ground-game has been shot, the dog is expected to take the line or foot-scent to where the game was shot. If the game runs, this line becomes a warm blood scent, which the dog should then follow until he obtains the retrieve. Where the runner is a rabbit, it may manage to kick itself down a hole, and when a dog fails on such a retrieve the judge will investigate where the line was lost and, if holes are present, the dog will not be penalized. Rabbits are not the only runners to disappear down holes, however, and many a running pheasant has been known to take refuge underground or in a drain. Should your dog be on such a runner and then seems to go rabbiting, it is a good bet that the pheasant has gone to ground.

The distance over which a dog is sent for a retrieve is often dependent on the type of countryside and position of the Gun who shot the bird. Some Guns also allow the bird to continue flying to what they consider a more sporting distance before they shoot, which can result in more runners. In a spaniel trial, where the emphasis is on hunting, handlers like the birds to be dead. One very knowledge-able land owner who generously gives his ground for trials was heard to tell a Gun who had not shot at a trial before, 'The bird is flushed, it's up, it's down, it's dead. The sport is in the dog work, not the shooting!'. The shooting that day was some of the best I have ever seen at a spaniel trial and gave every dog an opportunity of retrieving successfully.

Occasionally game will be shot by a back Gun or Gun in the wings. This will not have been marked by the dog but the judge should provide every opportunity for you to succeed. Long, blind retrieves are uncommon in spaniel trials and the judges will take you and your dog to within a reasonable distance of the retrieve before asking you to complete it. On an open-type piece of ground, you can expect to be asked to complete a longer unseen than if the cover is thick and possibly game-holding.

If the first dog fails on a retrieve, the second dog will be called across to make an attempt at it. If this dog succeeds in obtaining the retrieve, the first dog will be discarded. Where neither of the dogs succeed in collecting the retrieve, the judges will walk foward to look for the game themselves. If the game is found, both dogs will be discarded. If the shot game is not found, the dogs will be allowed to continue, but the first dog down on the retrieve will be downgraded. If the second dog had succeeded, he would have been credited with an eye wipe. In a retriever trial, this can bring a dog up into the frame, but in a spaniel trial this retrieve must not colour the judgement of the judges who will ensure that hunting skills take precedence over retrieving. A poor hunting dog would not be allowed to win because he had made an excellent retrieve. A spaniel will win a trial on his hunting ability as this is the main consideration of the judges, but the most common causes of elimination occur during the retrieve.

In a Novice trial, the Guns are asked not to shoot any game that is flushed while a dog is out on a retrieve. In an Open trial, shooting flushed game while the dog is retrieving is acceptable. I personally do not think that this is a good idea and some Guns at Open trials do not continue to shoot when this happens. If a dog is out on a retrieve and a bird that has been flushed is shot and falls near him, it is likely that he will pick this. If the game he was originally sent for happened to be a runner, the dog will have wasted time picking the newly shot game and allowed the bird a greater chance of escape, making his job even more difficult. This situation can also lead to the creation of bad habits such as the dog running about picking game that has fallen and not returning neatly to hand with each one. It is also possible that the dog may begin to run in to shot; there is nothing to stop him doing so in these circumstances and, in the trial, the handler cannot get out to the dog and correct him.

When both judges have seen all the dogs, they compare notes and look for their best dog or dogs. It sometimes happens that they both agree and one dog comes out on top. More commonly, they have different top dogs or a group of dogs have similar grades. In this case, a run off is carried out. If one dog has come out on top but a number of dogs are equal for the places, these are run off and the top dog is kept to one side. In Novice trials, game is not usually shot in the run off. In Open trials, the judges decide whether game will be shot according to the amount of game shot in the main part of the trial and the number of dogs in the run off – if there is a large number of dogs, shooting more game will help the decision as it will increase the amount of judgeable work to be done by the dog.

In a run off, the judges will be watching the dog's style, body movement, tail action, pace and natural quartering ability; in addition they will be observing the amount of whistle the handler is using and help he is giving the dog. In a run off, the judges ask for the two dogs running each time to keep as close together as possible, even overlap, so that the work can be more easily compared. The judges look for tidy, methodical work requiring little handler control, a dog who has pace and style and hunts his ground in such a way that you are excited by it and always hoping for the shot – in brief, an eye-catcher.

Once the Judges have made their decision, the Chief Steward will tell you that it is all over and you can make your way back to the meeting point. If you are the one who has been skilled and lucky enough to win, be prepared to give a vote of thanks to the judges.

SOME PERSONAL THOUGHTS

It does not seem all that long ago that I entered my first trial, possibly because time flies as you get older. Although I am no longer a beginner, I am constantly learning from people and dogs. That is what we should all be doing, learning from our own and other people's experiences. But how often do we take note of the lessons? Initially, my trialling was with spaniels but, since then, I have diversified, some will say progressed, to include retrievers. Although competitions for these dogs differ in the way they are run, there are still common elements of things to do and not to do.

When I look back to those early days when *I* had the best dog in the country (at least, in my mind he was) I must have appeared to other triallers and dog people as a cocky little know-all. I had won small local tests with the dog, I had given demonstrations of gundog training and handling and the dog was envied by my shooting friends because he worked well in the shooting field. So here I was, an 'expert', in my first trial and quickly being

The presentation of the awards is usually done by the host.

put out because the dog gave tongue (well, it was only a little yip!). He only did it occasionally but he did it then – this taught me my first lesson and I never entered him in another trial. Always make sure that you and your dog are ready for trialling and that your dog has none of the cardinal sins: giving tongue, hard-mouth, running in, refusing to retrieve, or being out of control. Do not run your dog in trials unless he is good enough – there are few enough places in trials for those dogs who are.

So before entering any competition, know what is expected of you and your dog. Your dog should have been brought up to a standard where you feel confident you will be able to handle the majority of situations faced. I often hear the comment that a trial is not a training ground, and this comment is particularly poignant when one hears statements such as 'Oh, he hasn't had a pheasant before' or 'Must I remove his lead during drives?'

But in trials, as in the shooting field, you encounters new situations which you may not have been able to meet before. The handler who is constantly thinking of all the difficult situations that can be encountered and who considers the dog unable to handle them will never get started. If in doubt about the standard of your dog and yourself for competition, ask someone who knows.

Study and familiarize yourself with the rules of the competition: it really is daft to have a good run only to be marked down because you have stepped over the mark. Judging certainly makes you aware of the rules, through necessity, but a novice does not have that experience under his belt. Obtain a set of rules from the Kennel Club and talk to experienced judges within your local club. One particular thing that I find so important is to arrive early for the trial. This gives you time to settle down, particularly after a long journey. Your dog will be able to answer the call of nature, you will be able to do likewise, and then you can make yourself known to the trial organizers. Being rushed creates all kinds of problems, the most obvious being additional stress. This transfers itself to your dog and therefore the whole team is not at its best.

Some triallers give their dog some basic work prior to a trial. Do make sure you are not exercising or practising on the trial ground! It is debatable whether this pre-trial work is good or bad. Too much can tire your dog mentally or may even create too much excitement. Certainly, you will not be able to add to the training of your dog in the short period prior to the competition. If he does not know by now, you cannot expect to perform miracles. A little 'dressage', however, may not come amiss. It reminds the dog of who is in charge and, more important,

helps to settle the nerves of both of you.

Get to know your dog and yourself and decide what is going to give you the best start. I have found that arriving early gives me time to calm down after the journey. For me, the best way of calming down is just being with my dog, walking him on the lead or sitting with him. This also calms him down and, in my opinion, we both end up in the right frame of mind. I do not know whether I do things in the same way each time for good luck, but I do feel that routine is good for the dog. A routine way of doing things breeds confidence in the dog through familiarity and an understanding of what is coming next. In this way, your dog becomes as mentally prepared as yourself. A big 'don't' at this stage is not to let your dog run about all over the place without any control. The owner of the ground may

Do not forget to collect your armband.

Ready for the 'Off'. Dogs on leads.

consider it bad manners and other handlers could resent your dog's being a nuisance to theirs, particularly prior to the trial. If your dog is a bitch, do make sure that she has not come into season – you will not be the most popular person otherwise.

When you arrive at the trial ground, park carefully and considerately if car parking is not marked. Let the organizer know you have arrived and ask where you can exercise your dog. You will be given a card that gives details of the stake, together with a list of the runners, and an armband with your number. Some societies also have a large number which you carry and give to an official when you are in the line; he then displays this on a number board to let spectators know which handler and dog is in action. Your armband should be attached to your left arm and, if you are running two dogs, only one armband should be displayed at

a time – make sure it is the right one!

Before the trial starts, the organizer will call for your attention and give you instructions relevant to the trial. Alterations may have been made to the card because dogs have been withdrawn or substituted after it had been printed and you will be given this information. Some trials will stop for lunch, others will go through, in which case, it is advisable to carry a snack with you. The most important thing to remember is that you are a guest of the shooting hosts and, as such, depend on their generosity to support our sport. Therefore, if there are any restrictions or details which they request to be observed, be sure to listen to them and act accordingly.

Time is another important factor in the trial. I can remember, when I first started going to training classes, a very good tip I was given: 'Give yourself and your dog time to think'. Whatever you are asked to

167

Lunch may have to be carried with you and eaten on the run.

do, do not rush into it unless the situation demands quick action. If you are getting hot under the collar or your dog is having problems, particularly on a retrieve, stop the dog, take a deep breath, think, and then take action. Panic is only successful when luck is on your side. Ignore the work of your co-competitors and run your dog at your pace ensuring that the job is done well. The judge will be wanting you to perform well so give yourself the opportunity of doing so by not trying to change your style. In spaniel trials you may find that the other competitor in the line starts to pull ahead of you. It could be that the other dog works faster or is not covering the ground well enough. The danger there is that game could be missed. The judges will ensure that the dogs keep together as much as possible, asking for the leading dog to wait until the other comes level. So work well and at your pace; let the judges manage the trial.

Nerves are bound to be there on the big day; they will never completely disappear however many trials you tuck under your belt. Try to control them, but it is my feeling that the adrenalin produced can heighten the concentration, impart itself to your dog and create a total team working at peak performance. How you control your nerves is up to you – good-luck charms, start routines, deep breathing, whatever – but do not lose concentration. Always keep that invisible communication lead between you and your dog. The day you do not experience nerves could lead you into sloppiness. You will not be the only person with nerves. Nervousness manifests itself in many different ways, so be aware of the feelings of other competitors and be understanding with them. I have seen competitors who tuck themselves well to the rear and do not involve themselves at all, resenting

At some trials, number boards are carried to let spectators know which dogs are running.

any intrusions. Others become too verbal or jocular, sometimes playing on your own nerves – my problem many times I fear! So if I am getting on your nerves, politely move away and settle yourself once more for the work in hand.

The moment you move forward into the 'Battle Front', you will need to be at the peak of concentration, and quite complex concentration it is too. The judge, the Guns, the ground, the game but most important your dog – concentrate on your dog. Once the trial is under way for you and your dog, the only person who should share your world is the judge. Listen to the judge and, if in doubt, ask. Were you asked to send your dog? Are you clear where the bird fell or which bird is required? Work your dog to the best of your ability, reading him and the messages transferred to you at every stage.

Gamesmanship does rear its head in competition and some degree of it may be successful, but the experienced judge has seen it all before and will recognize any move to take unfair advantage. As one judge told me, 'I wasn't born yesterday – there are very few tricks I haven't seen or sometimes even tried!' I have seen retrievers' ears held during a drive at a trial and have also heard of tails being held firmly to the ground by a foot strategically placed. Clever, maybe, but if caught out, do not expect sympathy.

Running your dog in competition is bound to involve you in a variety of situations, some you will have experienced before and some will be totally new. Some will present difficulties such as an awkward retrieve, or a particularly difficult piece of ground to work. Accept these difficulties as part of the game – every competitor will experience them in one form or another, the same as good and bad luck. In the end, I have found

169

'The Talk Shop'. Competitors and spectators discuss dogs and performances.

that it all balances out and if you and your dog are the right team you will make your own luck, sometimes even out of bad luck.

Trialling folk are generally a chatty and friendly bunch and enjoy sharing some of their knowledge and experiences. Do beware of the 'mine of information' trialler, however, who may appear to know it all but really has had no more experience than you. Such people can really fill you with concern, and even fear, if you accept everything they say, although sometimes I think that is their intention. The real founts of knowledge, I have found, tend to be quiet until approached when they will speak with a modesty which belies their depth of understanding and wisdom. I suppose it goes without saying that you should not set yourself up as the fount of knowledge; even at a Novice trial for novice dogs, the handlers will consist of many experienced and pro-fessional trainers. Most of these will listen to you politely and then place you in their minds as being the know-all newcomer.

The talk amongst the group of spectators and waiting competitors is usually very entertaining and good value in itself. Other trials, people, dogs, ground, plus the usual discussion topics, are aired. The world is put to rights and, by being involved, we may feel as though we have made a contribution to the day. But has any damage been done? The trials world depends on the generosity of many people, but particularly on the land and shoot owners who give their ground, game and time to help us enjoy the sport. Most of us have had experience of the competitor who comes out of the line after running a dog – things have not gone quite right, the competitor feels cheated, disappointed and needs to find a way to save face. 'The b**!!** Guns couldn't shoot an ostrich off a barn door at ten yards', or similar, is often heard. The waiting group laugh, realizing the comment is made in the heat of the moment with no real intention of offending. But the wife of one of the Guns hears it differently. Many comments, even innocent ones, can easily be misinterpreted and, although we should not always have to hang our words out for inspection before uttering them, I sometimes feel a little mental check prior to making them public would not come amiss.

Criticism is one of the easiest things. With hindsight, anyone can be critical and in many cases even hindsight is not necessary. The criticism given in the majority of cases is not justified and has been based on insufficient evidence. We may be looking for a way out for ourselves or our friends, a saving of face, or even just something to talk about. Unjustified criticism, particularly of a destructive nature, can be very damaging – individuals can take criticism very personally. So if you want a rule, do not criticize (particularly anything to do with the ground, the Guns or the host). Whatever you think, they have all given with the very best of intentions and in the interest of our sport. Always have in the back of your mind that we are the guests of our host and derogatory comments about anything to do with the host are not acceptable.

The whole atmosphere of a competition is something to be savoured. There is a sense of occasion, a need to succeed and demonstrate to others that you and your dog are a team to reckon with. If you do not win, it is not failure – excuses are not required. Reasons may need to be looked at and where deficiencies are obvious in dog or handler, these should be overcome, if possible, in readiness for the next time. Winning is great, the exhilaration, pride and feeling of euphoria that sweeps over you is one of life's memorable moments, quickly to be replaced by nerves when you are asked to give a vote of thanks to the judges. Whoever said 'winning isn't important, it's playing the game that counts' cannot have done much winning because it is magnificent. Winning means that on that day, you and your dog came through as the best in the judges' opinion. On that day, you had the opportunity, skill, ability, style and luck to make it to Number One. But remember that on another day it could quite easily be someone else.

13 Your Dog – Your Partner in the Game

KEEPING IT ALL GOING

A dog is with you all year round, not just in the shooting season, which tends to be all too short and go too quickly. Unlike other shooting equipment, your dog cannot be cleaned, oiled and put away until next season. But the off-season months can be valuable in providing you with the opportunity to reach new heights in the training and handling of your dog and in doing so keeping him, and often yourself, fit.

Dogs do seem to remember their training from year to year, provided nothing has been done to break the good habits and instil the bad. They do, however, become rusty and certainly they can lose condition and fitness. When the dog lives in the house, it is quite easy for him to become more dominant and independent, even wilful, if you are not consistent in your commands and expectations of response. If the exercising of the dog is left to a member of the family who does not know how to handle him and who may spoil any training that has been done, no matter how hard you work at putting right the wrong, you may never do so. If you really get to know and understand your dog, you will be able to determine how much leeway you can give him, how much freedom and how relaxed you can be in social situations. Some dogs, like children, will take advantage

and others will behave like angels. Often their good behaviour and your ability to have complete trust in them, is because you have done the basic training and socializing correctly.

In this book, I have described some advanced training exercises you can carry out. Basic training and exercises were explained in the earlier book, *Working Gundogs*. Never be too proud to go back to basic training in order to reinforce a

A day in the company of a good dog is always a happy one.

172

There is considerable pleasure in having a dog who brings back the goods.

lesson you want the dog to learn. By gradually building up the dog's ability a little bit at a time throughout the spring/summer break, you will be well prepared for the next season. It may be that you can also keep the dog up to scratch with the occasional foray on pigeons or rabbits. To do this, he may need some additional skills and you can prepare him for this. Generally, however, if your dog is obedient, under control and able to be handled, there should be few jobs that you cannot approach without a high degree of confidence.

A CONTINUOUS PROCESS

Your dog, like you, will never stop learning, whether it is through the training you give him or the experiences in the field. Learning and developing is a never-ending process and it is quite surprising how much more a dog learns as he gets older. Dogs seem to know things by intuition and instinct, which you would not normally expect. A specialist dog, such as one who accompanies the professional pigeon shooter, gets a limited range of experience very regularly and will quickly learn the routines. The dog of all trades, who many of us want to own, and who is only taken out once or maybe twice a week actually shooting, takes longer to gain the wide range of experience that will make him into a practical companion.

When a dog begins to bring back the goods and, in doing so, occasionally proves you wrong, you begin to appreciate the old saying, 'Trust your dog'. When you can relax, knowing that the dog is working for you and that there is a mutual confidence, you know you have a true partnership. I have been told by a few shooting dog owners that you only get one memorably good dog in your life. This should not be the case – every dog is different but through good training and thoughtful development of your relationship, they can all be memorable in their own way and be valued companions and friends. Build a partnership on mutual trust, confidence and respect and your days together in the field will become days to remember.

Index